6

Legends of the Lost

Legends of the Lost

Editor: Peter Brookesmith

BLITZ EDITIONS

398.2/

Material in this publication previously appeared in the weekly
partwork The Unexplained © 1980-83

© Orbis Publishing Ltd 1984, 1991

Published in this edition 1991 by Blitz Editions
an imprint of Bookmart Ltd
Registered number 2372865
Trading as Bookmart Limited
Desford Road, Enderby, Leicester LE9 5AD

Printed in Czechoslovakia
ISBN 1-85605-082-3
50839

Contents

Introduction

THERE ARE FEW THINGS more entertaining, to the historian who has few romantic illusions about the past, than listening to people rambling on about how much happier folk were in the good old days. There can hardly be an era in history that someone, somewhere does not believe was the great Golden Age. Some people look upon Victorian England, with its gin-shops, workhouses and heartless factory owners, as the height of human achievement, while others yearn for the simple life and wide open spaces of frontier days, when cowboys froze to death in the saddle and people were driven insane by the howling of the wind on the plains. Some people talk about the Second World War as if there were nothing so uplifting as the wail of an air raid siren or the scream of a *kamikaze* pilot's plane hurtling toward some hapless aircraft carrier below. The British, who have suffered an awful lot of history, are particularly adept at translating the grim and distant past into a rosy dream.

Perhaps the most remarkable of these transformations is the romanticisation of the medieval period into 'merrie England': the almost magic alteration of a diseased, poverty-stricken, politically unstable and threatened existence into an endless round of fine weather, wholesome food, smiling minstrels and noble knights. Never mind the plague, the beggars and the occasional nose-clipping: play music, and bring on the plump and comely wenches.

While we must keep a sense of reality, however, it is of course also true that no period of history has been filled with unmitigated gloom or unrelieved pain. What is curious and intriguing is the universal desire of humanity to make the past perfect – and, because perfect, an inspiration to the present. And in many cases this extraordinary process has actually been carried out successfully: time and again we find examples of societies that have drawn their coherence, their emotional and psychological stability, from a glorification of some period of their past. There is little doubt that the legends of King Arthur, for instance – actually inventions of troubadours and French monks – were an enormous force in uniting the British people during the medieval period, helping them to make a common future by inspiring them with the vision of a brilliant past. And for all its chicanery, shenanigans and lawlessness, the old West and its much revered qualities of self-reliance and freedom still speak to the American entrepreneurial spirit.

What role, then, do myths of a Golden Age play in our own society? Myths of a time when the world was young, in lands that, like Atlantis, have long since disappeared? What of the rumours that ancient man was master of a highly sophisticated technology, that dragons once stalked the Earth, or that beings from outer space visited us long ago, bestowed their wisdom and departed?

Perhaps the only thing that links this disparate group of myths is that, while they appear to be concerned with the past, their function is actually to illuminate some aspect of the present. The fact that each legend sheds light on a different facet of human existence is perhaps responsible for their variety: some, like the legend of Atlantis, are complex and shot through with a philosophy that amounts almost to a religion, while others, like the ubiquitous dragon legends, are accretions around a very simple story. The likely sources and inspirations for a fabulous, fire-breathing winged creature lie with the lizards and scorpions of the East, and the fantastical legends told about them by early explorers; it is small wonder that peoples around the world have spun tales of such wondrous animals, and that in some cases whole systems of thought have been founded on this remarkable, tantalising image. Indeed, its circling, spiralling form has been regarded as in some way representing the very forces of the Earth, sustainer of life, itself.

The roots and purpose of the Atlantis legends are less easily dealt with. That is in their modern aspect: the earliest recorded account is in the writings of Plato in the 4th century BC. The latter-day account of Atlantis is much more elaborate than that given by Plato, and has been built up largely through the reports of psychics claiming to have visions of the fabled civilization. Thus it is that we are authoritatively told by such sensitives about the wonders of Atlantean technology, public sanitation and philosophy. Not, however, that all this availed the super-race much, for predictably they became corrupt and idle in the wake of so much power and leisure and blew themselves to smithereens, probably – so the legend goes – by abusing nuclear power.

Given those bare bones of the plot – essentially a moral drama – it seems absurd to construct an argument based on archaeology and the geology of the ocean bed to refute the physical reality of an enormous continent in mid-Atlantic that suddenly and dramatically vanished. To those to whom the myth and the moral of Atlantis are real, such projects are, literally, immaterial. Ancient Chinamen made a moral reality of dragons by behaving as if dragons existed. In much the same way it is irrelevant whether or not Moses actually climbed up Mount Sinai or Jesus was really born in a stable in Bethlehem: enough people have behaved as if they did that, even were it to be proved otherwise tomorrow, such things might just as well have taken place. And so, I believe, it is with the myth of Atlantis.

For what, after all, does it amount to? Something uncannily akin to the story of our own times, or at any rate what many people fear for the future of today's society: a community of people of enormous talent and great achievement in the arts, in civilised living, in science, who lose their sense of moral direction and destroy themselves. The recent addition (by, of course, 'psychic messengers') of nuclear power into the Atlantean equation only reinforces the urgent suspicion that this is a moral fable for the present, not a representation of the past.

It is, of course, part of the fascination of lost civilisations that they *are* lost – that they remain only as glimpses and rumours, suggestive and tantalising. They have something of the aura of ruined houses, of ghost towns and deserted villages. The mysterious edifices that still stand in the Americas, Africa and southeast Asia are just that – insubstantial cities of echoes and shadows. And here too is evidence of another theme that threads its way through this corner of myth: that of self-destruction.

This is worth bearing in mind in any attempted analysis of, on one hand, the use to which the legends of Atlantis or King Arthur have been put by escapists and, on the other, what the stories are really trying to tell us. The Victorians were good at adding sugar icing to the medieval period and, in particular, the Arthurian myth. There is a movement abroad in our own time that claims to be the herald of a New Age in which, in spirit if not in fact, Atlantis will be seen to rise again. Atlantis is seen as a magical kingdom in which art and science, the objective and the intuitive, existed in synergetic harmony. But such a view seems a wilfully fanciful distortion of the original moral fable of Atlantis.

Similarly, the story of King Arthur as told by Sir Thomas Malory – gentleman, jailbird and literary genius – is commonly celebrated as an epic of the triumph of civilised values over barbarism, of justice and nobility over brute force and self-interest. To the extent that the Round Table represents a spiritual elite in search of the Holy Grail, this is true. Yet at the centre of Arthur's superb achievement there is a sickness: the adulterous love of Lancelot and Guinevere, which in the end splits apart all that Arthur has so painfully constructed over the years. There is another ingredient here, too: the inescapable operations of fate, for Arthur is forced to act against Lancelot and Guinevere by his natural son Mordred, whom he begot in an unwitting, indeed innocent, act of incest in his youth. That is a bleak irony worthy of ancient Greek tragedy. Like the Atlantis legend, Arthur's story contains powerful reminders of the intertwining of good and evil and the fragility of one's power to control one's destiny despite all effort and good intention, that are typical of ancient Greek literature.

No less fascinating is the way in which these myths and legends – still so powerful, however they are interpreted, to the modern mind – have come into being, and the essays that follow have concentrated largely on their roots and origins.

One subject of modern interest dealt with here – although apparently an objective matter of the study of prehistory – is no less the stuff of which myths are made. There has been a prevalent opinion – a kind of negation of a Golden Age myth – that the life of primitive man was nasty, brutish and short and that he can have achieved nothing in the way of technology. And yet there is an extraordinary catalogue of peculiarly anachronistic artefacts that have turned up in places all over the world where they really ought not to belong – stainless steel from seams of coal millions of years old, for instance, or human footprints among those that were unmistakably made by dinosaurs. Such oddities and anomalies have been seized upon by, among others, those who not only reject the accepted principles of evolution, but would like to prove that the process of evolution didn't happen at all. Whether or not the case against Darwin and his disciples is actually strengthened in this way is open to doubt, but these objects persist in turning up and perplexing science.

But there is another somewhat wayward 'explanation' for these artefacts: that they were left behind by passing extra-terrestrials on occasional visits to the developing Earth. That is possible – or at least it can't be proved to be impossible – but such a slender likelihood has become the basis of a systematic re-interpretation of history undertaken by, among others, the notorious Erich von Däniken. This school has created a myth for our times, and a careful study of it tells us much about modern humanity's opinion of itself (von Däniken's books have, after all, sold millions of copies).

It's worth saying in passing that von Däniken is only the best-known of these writers (and now by far the richest) and that most of his ideas are borrowed from others less skilled at self-promotion. Nonetheless, it is strange that so many people seem to believe in the inherent stupidity of the human race – for that is the assumption that underlies von Däniken's theory. Ancient man is deemed to have been too simple-minded to discover fire, or to have learned to build cities, while more developed civilisations were apparently incapable of the feats of constructing the pyramids or Stonehenge. Instead, he had to enlist the help of benificent beings from outer space. And whatever use mankind may later have put these buildings to, they exist – so von Däniken and his followers allege – as beacons and signal stations for the aliens, who have found the secret of tapping 'earth energy' for their own purposes. Quite why these spacemen were so chary of using electronic aids as the rest of us do is never explained, and the arrogance displayed in assuming that our ancestors had virtually no technological skills is truly staggering. It is surprising, really, given the astonishing development of technology in the 20th century alone, that von Däniken has not suggested that Marconi, the Wright Brothers and Albert Einstein were secretly in touch with the same intergalactic gang. Or perhaps they were even aliens themselves.

The past is more interesting than either romantics or fantasists can make it by their relentless selections of truth, half-truths and innuendo – and a good deal more mysterious as well, as the essays in this book will show in a wealth of detail.

PETER BROOKESMITH

The fabled, fire-breathing dragon

The notion of a winged, fire-breathing serpent has haunted men's minds for centuries. ANNA PAVORD begins her analysis of the power that the mythical dragon wields in the imagination of both East and West

THE DRAGON winds its serpentine way through the legends of all countries of the Old World and many of the New. A whole gallery of the world's heroes – Perseus, Marduk, Hercules, Siegfried, St George, Beowulf – have fought it and killed it, but it refuses to die. It lives on as a folk memory: a huge, scaly creature, reptilian, and usually winged in a leathery, bat-like way. It breathes fire, guards treasure, haunts pools – and its blood is more venomous than that of any other creature imaginable.

New myths continually reinforce the essential elements of the old legend. Smaug, Tolkien's dragon, guards a mountain hoard, 'countless piles of precious things, gold wrought and unwrought, gems and jewels and silver red-stained in the ruddy light.' The dragons of Anne McCaffrey's science-fiction books feed on firestone, which combines with acids in the digestive system to produce poisonous phosphines. 'When the dragons belched forth gas, it would ignite in the air into ravening flame.' C. S. Lewis's Narnian dragon, the metamorphosed Eustace from *The voyage of the Dawn Treader*, discovers the joys of flight climbing out of his lair in the valley. 'He began the climb with a

Below: Tolkien's dragon, Smaug, from *The Hobbit*, undertakes the traditional employment of dragons – guarding a mound of fabulous treasure

jump and as soon as he jumped he found that he was flying.'

Christian tradition has made the dragon into a devil figure, the embodiment of all evil, 'the dragon, the old serpent' cast out from heaven by the archangel Michael – but it was not always so. The true dragon was an ambivalent creature, combining both good and bad qualities. It was a creature to be propitiated with human sacrifice, a guardian of watery places – the giver, if it chose, of rain. It was also a symbol of regeneration. To slay the dragon was to refertilise the earth, and this symbolic ritual was perpetuated in folk drama and annual rites in both the Eastern and the Western world.

The dragon is a stock character of the mummers' plays – killed by St George, brought to life again by the doctor. In Sicily an effigy of a dragon was carried in procession on St George's Day, along with two huge loaves. At the end of the festival, the loaves were broken into little pieces and every farmer buried his part in his field to ensure the fertility of his crops.

In Bavaria the drama of the dragon-slaying was played out at midsummer. The critical part of this ritual was St George's piercing of a bladder of blood carried inside the dragon effigy. The blood was mopped up

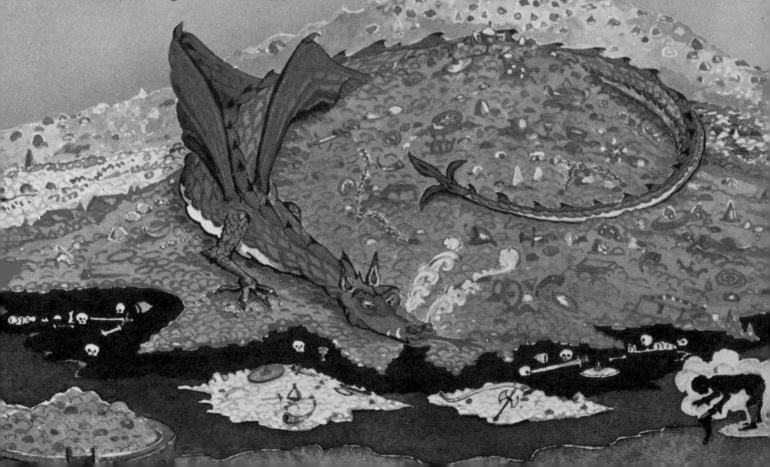

fascinated loathing characteristic of the Western man's view of the dragon:

> Up from his shoulders
> there grew a hundred snakes' heads,
> those of a dreaded dragon,
> and the heads licked with dark tongues
> and from the eyes on
> the inhuman heads fire glittered
> from under the eyelids.
> From all his heads fire flared
> from his eyes' glancing;
> and inside each one of these horrible
>   heads
> there were voices
> that threw out every sort of horrible
>   sound.

This dragon, Typhon, fought a terrible battle with Zeus, crippling him with a sickle. Hermes, messenger of the gods, healed Zeus who then chased Typhon all through Thrace into Sicily, where he finally buried him under Mount Etna.

Typhon was the father of a formidable brood that provided many of the monstrous creatures of Greek legend – the Chimera, the Nemean lion, the eagle that ate Prometheus's

by the spectators and later spread over the flax fields to help the harvest.

The Chinese New Year is celebrated with huge dragon effigies of paper and bamboo, which are carried in procession through the streets. The dragon is mutable and it is ubiquitous. Its influence is pervasive. Creation myths of many cultures regard it as the beginning of all things.

A Babylonian epic, the *Enuma elish*, tells how, in the beginning, the mighty god Marduk fought and killed the great dragon Tiamat, embodiment of the original watery chaos, and how, after his victory, he created heaven and earth:

> He split her like a shellfish in two parts,
> Half of her he set up and sealed it as the
>   sky,
> Pulled down the bar and posted guards.
> He bade them to allow not her waters to
>   escape.

The other half became the earth and so confusion was reduced to order, a cosmos was made from chaos.

An Indian myth, found in the *Rig Veda*, a collection of Sanskrit hymns dating from about 1000 BC, tells how the valiant god Indra conquered a great dragon called Vrítra that had sealed up all the life-giving waters of the earth. Indra killed the monster, releasing the water, which flowed once more in a thousand springs, streams and rivers. This conflict was seen not as a once and for all victory for the god, but as a battle that had to be faced and fought over and over again to bring monsoon rains out of drought.

The first classical dragon was Typhon, a monstrous animal of Greek mythology, associated with volcanoes and high winds (hence typhoon). The ancient Greek poet Hesiod described it in *Theogony* with the

Above: on Christmas Day 1849 at the Free Trade Hall in Manchester, a member of the Mechanics' Institute (suitably attired as the patron saint of England) slew the dragon before a crowd of 5000 merrymakers. After the dragon was thus despatched, the dancing could begin

Right: St Michael and the Dragon, by Bartolomeo Bermejo, dating from 1470. Here the dragon is seen as a demon, with St Michael as the champion of Heaven

liver, and the many-headed dragon killed in the second of the twelve labours assigned to the Greek superman-hero Hercules.

This creature, the Hydra, lived under a plane tree terrorising the people who lived round the Lernaean swamp near Argos. It was not only malicious and venomous, but also self-regenerating. Hercules called on his charioteer, Iolaus, to burn the stump of each neck as he sliced through the heads, and in this way prevented new heads appearing. He then dipped his arrows into the creature's blood, tipping them with deadly poison.

Ladon the dragon was another of Typhon's offspring, also defeated in battle against Hercules, who flung it into the sky where it still glitters as the constellation Draco. Ladon guarded the Golden Apples of immortality that the goddess Hera, wife of Zeus, had received as a marriage gift, and was an early representative of the dragon as custodian of treasure – a recurring motif of dragonlore. The Golden Fleece sought by Jason and the Argonauts was also guarded by a dragon, a terrible beast that never slept.

The dragon as guardian also occurs

Left: the ancient Greek hero, Hercules, slays the many-headed dragon as the second of his 12 labours

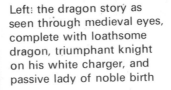

Left: the dragon story as seen through medieval eyes, complete with loathsome dragon, triumphant knight on his white charger, and passive lady of noble birth

Left: an Assyrian seal showing the hero Marduk about to kill the monster-dragon Tiamat, goddess of the sea and mother of all the gods

frequently in Old English, Norse and German mythology, together with the theme of hero versus monster, but both heroes and dragons differ from their glittering classical forbears. The philosophy that filled the Northern European sagas and epics, the *Nibelungenlied* of Germany, the *Eddas* of Iceland, the Anglo-Saxon *Beowulf*, was sombre and pessimistic.

The heroes were on the sides of the gods, but the gods, although on the right side, were not on the winning side. The dragons had still to be met and fought and killed, but there was no possibility of victory, for they seem to represent the final heroic test of courage, the facing of one's inevitable death. So Sigurd, the Norse hero – who became Siegfried, the dragon-slayer of Wagner's *Der Ring des Nibelungen* (The ring of the Nibelungs) – dies after his epic encounter with Fafnir.

Beowulf, the hero of the Anglo-Saxon epic that bears his name, survives his first youthful encounter with a monster, the hideous Grendel, whom he kills, but in his old age has to face another, 'the primeval enemy that haunts the dusk: the scaly, malicious Worm which seeks out funeral mounds and flies burning through the night, wrapped about with flame, to the terror of the country folk. Its habit is to seek out treasure hidden in the earth and mount guard over the pagan gold, but, though ancient in years, it will profit nothing thereby.'

Abandoned by all his companions except his kinsman Wiglaf, Beowulf fights a terrible battle with the mound-hoarder. His patterned sword, the Naegling, fails him, his shield is shattered by the creature's searing breath but, at the third attack, Beowulf succeeds in ripping open the soft underbelly

of the monstrous dragon.

No more would the coiled Worm guard the hoarded treasure, for keen blades of hammered iron had destroyed it. The far-flying one had been mortally wounded, tumbled to earth beside its treasure house. No more would it spin through the air at dead of night to flaunt itself in its possession of the treasure for the hand of the king had felled it to the ground.

Beowulf, mortally wounded, dies with the dragon.

This story, which survives in its earliest form in an old English manuscript of about AD 1000, highlights another recurring feature of these legends – the dragon's vulnerability to iron, which it shares with fairies, vampires and evil manifestations of all kinds.

The dragon also plays an important part in Celtic mythology: for the Celts, as for the Romans, the dragon became a national standard. A purple dragon ensign was the standard of the rulers of the Eastern Empire of Rome, and a Roman writer Marcellinus describes Constantius entering Rome surrounded by cohorts of soldiers bearing dragon effigies as three-dimensional standards, 'the wind whistling in their throats as if they had been alive, threatening destruction.'

The Celtic dragon is the red *Y Ddraig Coch*, adopted as a standard by Uther Pendragon, the father of King Arthur. Uther had seen a vision of a flaming dragon in the sky, and his soothsayers interpreted this as a sign that he would inherit his brother's kingdom. When this came about, Uther ordered two magnificent dragon standards to be made. The one he dedicated to Winchester Cathedral, the other he carried with him into battle as an omen of good fortune, of strength and power.

In Celtic literature, the word dragon was also used to denote a chief, and a *Pen-dragon* was a super-chief, elected in times of danger and war to be overall leader. This semantic

Above left: Islamic hero Rustem kills this dragon as the second of his seven trials

Above right: an illustration from a ballad book depicts one 'Moore of Moore Hall' showing his contempt for the Dragon of Wantley before slaying him in time-honoured fashion. The spectators watch the combat from a safe distance

Below: Aryan hero Siegfried kills one of mythology's great dragons – the monstrous Fafnir

muddle may account for some of the many dragon legends along England's border with Wales. The dragons that were slain may not have been reptilian monsters, but possibly the leaders of bands of Welsh marauders.

The martial dragon was evidently a goody – the only occasion when it was allowed to play such a role in Western mythology. In England's St George legend it is very definitely the baddy again. The dragon's insatiable appetite for maidens (preferably of noble birth, princesses best of all) is a primary element in this type of story, where the princess plays an important, though maddeningly passive, role. The basic scenario changes very little.

A wandering knight comes to a strange land and finds all the people mourning. The king and queen of that country are weeping on the ramparts of their castle. The land about the castle is bleak and barren, no lush grass, no bright flowers, only the broken and blackened stumps of trees long since dead. A dragon is ravaging the king's land and lots have been drawn to choose a human sacrifice of propitiation. The choice falls upon the king's own daughter, who is led out, decked with jewels and bound to the sacrificial stake.

The knight, anxious to add to his dossier of good deeds, offers to release the princess, but she begs him to leave. Only by her death can her father's land be saved. Willy-nilly, the knight determines to meet the dragon in combat. He attacks it as it approaches the princess and kills it by piercing it with his iron lance. Cartloads of treasure from the dragon's lair are brought back to the king's counting house. The knight marries the

princess and all live happily ever after.

This is an all-purpose maiden story, an archetype that illustrates recurring motifs. The details alter to suit local conditions.

Orthodox scholarship traces the St George story and other maiden myths back to the classical story of Perseus, who rescued the Ethiopian princess Andromeda from a sea-monster sent by Neptune.

There have been many interpretations of the St George legend. In a Christian allegory, the maiden represents the Church, rescued from the evil dragon of paganism by Christianity in the form of a knight/saint. Freudians arrange the symbols in a different pattern and arrive at an infinitely more erotic interpretation.

St George's dragon, the classical dragons, Beowulf's dragon are all of the first water, epic dragons. There is also, however, a host of lesser relatives, the serpents and worms that crop up with great regularity in collections of British folklore.

The legends follow in a homely way the tradition of the more famous hero-versus-monster tales, but they have much local detail. The dragon of Loschy Hill, like the Lambton Worm, was a self-joining monster,

Above: Linton Hill in Roxburghshire where the 'Linton Worm' had its lair

Left: the Ethiopian version of St George and the Dragon. Some think the real St George came from north Africa

Right: the Indian super-hero Indra rides into battle against the dragon Vritra on his war-elephant

Below: the slaying of the Lambton Worm, which had 'the power of reuniting any parts of its body that were divided.' The heir of Lambton put on a suit of armour studded with razor blades and lay in wait for the Worm on a crag in a river close to the dragon's lair. When the dragon attacked him, it was cut to pieces by the razor blades, and the river carried away the severed parts of the body, preventing them from rejoining

conquered eventually with the help of the hero's dog. As his master hacked away, the dog ran off with the pieces to prevent them joining up again. Sadly, the dragon's poisonous breath proved fatal to both master and dog.

The Linton worm terrorised a small parish in Roxburgh, Scotland, some time in the 12th century, destroying cattle and men indiscriminately. It was killed by a knight called Somerville of Lariston in an unusual way, a variation of the iron lance method. His lance was speared with a block of peat, dipped in burning pitch, and it was this fireball that burned out the dragon's entrails. The spiral ridges on Wormington Hill are said to have been made in the final death throes of the worm.

Altogether there are 50 different dragon tales recorded in British folklore. Worldwide there are thousands more. Why so many? What is the nature of the dragon's power? No explanation, however ingenious, satisfactorily accounts for the tenacity of these legends, or their fundamental immutability.

of villagers, who stabbed it with pitchforks.

Another British Museum document, the Bowes manuscript, describes an encounter with the Sockburn dragon, which terrorised a parish in County Durham in Saxon times:

> Sir John Conyers, Kt. slew that monstrous and poisonous vermin, wyvern, asp or werme, wh: had overthrown and devoured many people in fight for that the scent of the poison was so strong that no person might abyde it. And by the Providence of the Almighty God, the said John Conyers, Kt overthrew the sd. monster and slew it. . . .

Rational minds have, of course, explained away the story of the Sockburn dragon. Some say that the word 'dragon' was used as a symbol to describe a flood of the River Tees, which loops in a horseshoe round the village. Others interpret it as a tale of Danish raiders, who invaded many rivers of the north-east coast in boats with high serpent-carved prows.

It is not difficult to explain away dragons, but the fact that several different explanations are offered up for each dragon legend indicates a central weakness in the very process of explaining. The point is that the image of the dragon was so strong that it superseded all other images or words that might have been used in its stead. In the original account of the Sockburn Worm, Sir John did not divert a flood, or fight the Danes, or the devil, or even a giant. He fought a dragon.

A striking but fallacious argument for the physical existence of the dragon is put forward by Peter Dickinson in his book *The flight of dragons* (1979). He puzzled for a long time about the problem of how such a bulky creature could have flown. Even allowing for

Where have all the dragons gone?

What is the origin of the dragon legends that abound throughout the world? Are they simply stories invented by Man to explain events he did not understand – or are they somehow rooted in fact?

'THE DRAGON,' runs an entry in a Natural History published in 1776, is 'a most terrible animal, but most probably not of Nature's formation.' It seems that, in the Age of Reason, it was worth hedging one's bets. Perhaps the writer had in mind the story of the Essex serpent, which had been killed only a hundred years earlier in 1668 at Henham, north of Bishop's Stortford. It is commemorated in a carving at Henham church and in a contemporary pamphlet, now in the British Museum. A woodcut made at the same time shows it as a creature with no legs and a scaly skin with toad-like bumps. It was about 9 feet (3 metres) long and was killed by a band

Above: an artist's impression of a Viking attack on the British. Some people have tried to explain away the prevalence of dragon myths in Britain by interpreting them as stories of the Danish raiders who, in the eighth century, came in sailing ships with high dragon prows to attack the coastal towns and villages of north-eastern Britain. But is there, as others claim, more to the legends?

weight-saving strategies, he calculated that an average dragon body, based on different descriptions of the beast, must have weighed about 20,000 pounds (9000 kilograms). Giving the dragon a capacity for lift roughly equal to that of the bumblebee, which can lift $2\frac{1}{2}$ pounds of body weight for each square foot (0.17 kilograms per square centimetre) of wing, he arrived at a wing span for his average dragon of over 600 feet (180 metres). Physically this was impossible.

A chance viewing on television of the wreck of the airship *Hindenburg* in 1937 provided the catalyst for a radical reappraisal of the dragon problem. He concluded that dragons could fly because most of their bodies were hollow, and filled with a lighter-than-air gas; they needed an enormous body to hold enough gas to provide lift for the total weight of the beast; they did not need enormous wings, because they used them only for propulsion and manoeuvring; and they breathed fire because they had to. It was a necessary part of their specialised mode of flight.

Dickinson suggested, in defiance of all chemical possibility, that the inside of the dragon must have been a vast chemical reactor with hydrochloric acid, already present in the digestive systems of all vertebrates, reacting with calcium obtained from the bone structure to form hydrogen, a lighter-than-air gas. The dragon's bone must have been self-renewing, depending on a certain intake of limestone.

This metabolic process could not be completely shut down when the dragon was at rest, so from time to time it would need to vent surplus hydrogen. The safest way to do this would be to burn it off, with an ignition system probably depending on chemical rather than electrical means.

The theory also provides neat explanations for the essential features of dragons – their venomous blood and their predilection for princesses and treasure – and offers a tempting answer to a nagging problem, the absence of any true dragon fossils. 'Flight,' writes Dickinson 'was achieved by a controlled digestion of parts of the bone structure. When the dragon died, the control mechanism ceased to operate and the whole structure corroded.'

This concept of spontaneous liquefaction crops up in a report of an interview in Ireland that took place in July 1968 – years before Dickinson published his theory. F. W. Holiday was questioning a local resident about a dragon, sea monster, or *peiste* that, a generation earlier, had been found in a culvert near Lough Derrylea, Cross, County Clare. 'It couldn't wriggle itself through,' said the

Above: a carving on the porch of the church of St Mary the Virgin, Henham, commemorates the killing of the famous 'Essex serpent' in 1668

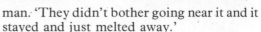

Below: a dragon from a Viking tombstone found in the churchyard of St Paul's Cathedral, London. Dragons formed an important part of Viking religious imagery

man. 'They didn't bother going near it and it stayed and just melted away.'

If one believes that the legend and fantasy surround a kernel of fact, then there is little doubt that the mythical dragon of countless tales is the successor of some real animal.

The pterodactyl has something of the dragon about it; so does the plesiosaur, a sea monster that hunted in our waters 150 million years ago. In the summer of 1980, the most complete skull and jawbones yet found of a plesiosaur were dug out of a claypit in Westbury, Wiltshire. It had about 80 teeth, the biggest 8 inches (20 centimetres) long, and the jaw suggested that the creature must have been 30 feet (9 metres) long.

Perhaps the dragon, having mastered the art of flight, escaped the consequences of the cataclysm that wiped out its saurian relatives. Its extinction (if it is extinct, for there are some who argue for its continued existence) came much later, the consequence of shrinking habitats and the unremitting hostility of its chief enemy, Man.

On a slightly different tack, Professor Carl Sagan accounts for the spread and consistency of dragon legends by saying that they represent a kind of fossil memory that has come down to us from the time of the dinosaurs, a general race memory inherited from our ancestors, who had to compete with these giant predators. In *The dragons of Eden* he writes:

The most recent fossil is dated at about sixty million years ago. The family of man (but not the genus *Homo*) is some tens of millions of years old. Could there have been man-like creatures who actually encountered *Tyrannosaurus Rex*? Could there have been dinosaurs that escaped the extinctions in the late Cretaceous period?

Although the idea of an overlap is necessarily speculative, the dragon as an image of some imperfectly remembered but traumatic saurian/simian conflict is a strong one.

The monks who wrote and illustrated the

bestiaries, popular and improving tracts of the Middle Ages, interpreted the dragon rather differently. Each creature in the bestiary illustrates some moral lesson. The phoenix is the symbol of resurrection, the panther is Christ, the dragon anti-Christ. In a typical story the panther dines, then sleeps for three days. When it wakes up, it belches and all the other animals follow its sweet breath. But the dragon, the panther's only enemy, hides away in fear of the breath, which can destroy it.

In the *Bestaire de Guillaume le Clerc de Normandie*, made between 1210 and 1211, the dragon fights with the elephant (which represents Adam), striking it with its tail and winding about its legs.

The Roman historian Pliny also commented on the enmity between dragon and elephant in his *Histories*, written in the first century AD:

India bringeth forth the biggest elephants and also the dragons that are continually at variance with them and evermore fighting, and those of such greatness that they can easily clasp and wind them around the elephants and withal tie them fast with a knot.

Pliny was one of the earliest of a long line of writers who believed in the dragon as a zoological actuality.

Edward Topsell, who wrote the *Historie of serpents* (1658), was another believer. His descriptions of dragons are precise and detailed, often accompanied by engravings showing the different types that he defines in the text, the serpent-dragon drawn next to its closest kin, the snake, a reptilian

Left: the jaw of a plesiosaur, a sea monster that has been extinct for 150 million years. This example, the most complete ever found, was dug out of a claypit in Westbury, Wiltshire, in the summer of 1980. The enormous plesiosaur has much about it that is reminiscent of the dragon, and Dr Carl Sagan has conjectured that dragon myths may represent an imperfect race memory of a conflict between humans and monsters of the Jurassic period

Below: a flying lizard, *Draco volans*, from the Indo-Malayan region. This creature can actually fly, or glide, on its webbed wings. But it is difficult to see how the dragon legends could have grown up around it, for it is only about 6 inches (15 centimetres) long

Right: St Martha and 'her' dragon, from an Italian woodcut of the 15th century. The biblical St Martha was the sister of Mary Magdalene and Lazarus, but in medieval times she became confused with another Martha, whose name was associated with a mysterious legend. It was said that she had been able to subdue a dragon that was ravaging the countryside near Tarascon in south-east France by sprinkling it with holy water. Tying her girdle around its neck, she led it over 10 miles (16 kilometres) to Arles, where it was killed

dragon accompanying a chameleon. 'Indian, Aethiopian and Phrygian dragons have very wide mouths,' he says 'through which they often swallow in whole fowls and beasts.' The Indian dragons he subdivides into two categories, the marsh dragon and the mountain dragon.

Their snouts are very strong, resembling the great ravening fishes; they have beards of yellow-golden colour, being full of bristles: and the Mountain dragons commonly have more deep eye-lids than the Dragon of the Fens. Their aspect is very fierce and grim and whensoever they move upon the earth, their eyes give a sound from their eye-lids, much like unto the tinkling of Brasse, and sometimes they boldly enter into the sea and take Fishes.

Topsell is equally precise about the medicinal properties of the dragon. The fat is a remedy for creeping ulcers, the head is good for curing a squint and the tongue, pickled in wine, will protect against 'Incubi, Succubi, or else Night-mares.'

The early cartographers also acknowledged the dragon's existence: 'It is alle deserte and fulle of Dragouns and grete serpentes.' They may possibly have been using it as a symbol for lands beyond their knowledge, but there is some evidence to suggest that for them the dragon was as real as the exotic giraffes and elephants that they crammed into the spaces between their boldly delineated rivers and their scatterings of castles.

Orthodox zoologists suppose that the existence of the mythical dragon amongst other perfectly credible animals in early maps and histories came about as a result of faulty

interpretation. It was in this way that Marco Polo's description of a Chinese alligator was turned by a contemporary artist into a very dragonish beast. Marco Polo described the alligator as a huge serpent with two short legs near the head, wide jaws and big, sharp teeth. It was the artist who added wings and a tail tipped with a miniature serpent head.

Some large snakes, particularly the boa constrictor or the python, have dragonish qualities. They can grow to 25 feet (7.5 metres) in length, and have the serpentine body of the dragon, though none of its appendages. In 1978, *The Times* carried a report from India about a python that half-swallowed a man. Villagers fought against

Above: an illustration from a medieval account of Marco Polo's travels. The dragon in the middle is based on an accurate description of the Chinese alligator – it is the artist who has added the wings and tipped the tail with a tiny serpent's head

Below: the elephant, representing Adam, fights with the dragon, representing the anti-Christ, in this illustration from a medieval bestiary

the snake and in the battle both python and victim died. Telling the story, the villagers afterwards used the word 'dragon' for the snake.

The flying lizards of the Indo-Malayan region actually bear the zoological name *Draco* and can fly, or rather glide, on webbed wings. The problem is that they are only about 6 inches (15 centimetres) long, and it is difficult to see how anything so small could have inspired the awe and fascination that has kept the dragon legends alive for so long.

A larger lizard, *Varanus komodoensis*, is popularly called the Komodo dragon. It grows up to 12 feet (3.5 metres) in length and looks reasonably dragonish, with a flat, ugly head, forelegs and a long, scaly body. However, it does not fly and its habitat is restricted to some Indonesian islands.

Crocodiles, alligators, snakes and lizards all have some reptilian features in common with the dragon, but none of them has enough to identify it positively as the source of the legend. One might as well try to prove that a lion is a dog because both are four-legged carnivores. If the dragon existed on this earth, then it seems more likely that it existed as a species in its own right. If it did not exist, then it is possible that it was created by men to explain or rationalise cosmic happenings or earthly forces that were far beyond their understanding or control.

The path of the dragon

The emperors of ancient China built their palaces on dragon paths – and the dragon symbol is also associated with many of Britain's ancient sites.

Above: a Japanese *tatsu*, or dragon, from a 19th-century watercolour. The *tatsu* was generally more serpentine than the Chinese dragon, and was regarded as a god of sea or river

THE EASTERN DRAGON is a quite different creature from its Western counterpart. The Eastern dragon is an infinitely more beneficent beast, living in the rain clouds, the sea, rivers, lakes, pools and springs. Dragon-slaying, one of the recurring motifs in Western dragonlore, has no equivalent in the Far East, for in Chinese philosophy the dragon acts as an essential link between earth and sky.

The Eastern dragon became an emblem of power, and the Chinese emperor sat on a dragon throne and wore dragon robes. Chinese dragons were also an essential ele-

ment in the ancient practice of geomancy, or *feng-shui*. A geomancer was an extraordinary sort of surveyor who, by dowsing and by calculations based on the stars, worked out where the cities, palaces and graves of the emperors should be placed so that they would gain the maximum benefit from the earth's magnetic currents. These currents could either be negative (*yin*) or positive (*yang*). The positive current was represented by a male dragon and followed the high places, the mountains and sharp peaks where the dragon lived. The routes by which he travelled from height to height were called *lung-mei*, dragon paths. It was important that a balance should be maintained between *yin* and *yang*, and all new buildings, roads or other disturbances of the natural balance had to be placed where they would harmonise with the 'local currents of the cosmic breath' – or serious consequences could result.

As the emperors grew more powerful in China, the geomancers also worked to channel the natural streams of earth energy and to direct them towards the imperial seat of government in Peking. These channels, imperial dragon paths, were carefully protected and no buildings were allowed along the lines, except those to do with the emperor and his family. The future success of a dynasty was said to rest in the geomancers' ability to choose the most advantageous and propitious place for the burial of its founder.

John Michell, who has written a great deal about *feng-shui* and *lung-mei*, believes that this knowledge of harmony between heaven and earth was once common all over the old world, the basis of many ancient religions that incorporate earth mothers and sky gods. He thinks that, not only in ancient China, but in Britain, France and other countries too, men chose for their sacred places sites that bore a direct relationship to an earth force.

These ancient sites   megaliths, stone circles, barrows, mounds – acted as conductors for this hidden energy and alignments between the sites called ley lines carried the force in a complex grid over Britain. Michell discovered that the dragon image seemed to be involved in certain British alignments that echoed the *lung-mei* of China.

One of these alignments marks the longest possible stretch of unbroken land in the south of England, starting in the west at St Michael's Mount in Cornwall, running through the ancient centres of both Glastonbury and Avebury and finishing on the east coast, north of Lowestoft. This line also corresponds exactly with the angle of sunrise on May Day.

Tracing the line from the west, Michell discovered a high incidence of dragon associ-

snout of the great hound traced out in the Somerset landscape – the hound that guards the Temple of the Stars, the Glastonbury zodiac. On the edge of Sedgemoor is the church of Othery St Michael, whose porchway is carved with a dragon.

From Othery the line runs on to Glastonbury, where the Tor now rises from an unlovely sea of red brick villas, but is still an extraordinary eminence in the Somerset flats. The chapel on the hilltop is dedicated to St Michael, and a spiral serpentine path leads up to the summit. The line passes just south of the parish of Stoke St Michael on its way to Avebury, where the huge Neolithic temple seems to represent a serpent. Two sinuous avenues of stones, each 50 feet (15 metres) wide and a mile and a half (2 kilometres) long, once extended from the great central circle. One curved south-east and ended in a small stone circle on top of Overton Hill, the head of the serpent. The other, now completely destroyed, but plotted on 19th-century maps as Beckhampton Avenue, reached out to the west, narrowing to form the serpent tail. A 12th-century font in the church at Avebury shows a bishop, book in hand, striking with his crozier at a winged

ations, carvings, legends, place names and churches dedicated to St George or St Michael. It seemed as if the church might have made these dedications to saints famed for dragon-slaying in an attempt to stamp out an old pagan religion centred around serpent- and dragon-worship, a veneration for some ancient power indicated by the megalithic monuments.

The western starting point of this great alignment, St Michael's Mount, is a dramatic rocky outpost off the Cornish coast that is also a sacred megalithic site. The line runs through the Hurlers on Bodmin Moor – three stone circles, the biggest 135 feet (40 metres) across, which legend represents as serpents metamorphosed by a Christian saint. St Michael's Church at Brent Tor on the edge of Dartmoor perches on top of an outcrop of black rock. St Michael's Church in the valley at Cadbury, further east in Devonshire, is overshadowed by a great causewayed camp. *A survey of Devon*, published in 1626, records a legend of a dragon that scoured the surrounding countryside from a lair at the top of the camp. Twenty miles (30 kilometres) away is the church of St Michael at Trull; a dragon was reputedly killed on nearby Castleman's Hill. A window on the south side of the church sanctuary shows three saints – George, Michael and Margaret – each slaying a different dragon.

Five miles (8 kilometres) on is Creech St Michael, followed by Lyng where dragons decorate both pew ends and windows in the church. The ruins of another St Michael's church stand at the summit of a conical artificial mound known as the Burrowbridge Mump. This ancient site also features as the

Many of the ancient sacred sites of Britain are linked by straight lines that seem to be connected with the image of the dragon-serpent. One runs from St Michael's Mount in Cornwall (top), through the Hurlers on Bodmin Moor (above) – which, legend tells, represent serpents turned to stone by a Christian saint. The line continues past three churches of St Michael the dragon-slayer before it reaches the ruined tower of St Michael's Church on Burrow Mump (right)

Above: the megalithic ring at Avebury, which marks a point of the great alignment that starts at St Michael's Mount in Cornwall

Left: a plan of Avebury Ring published by William Stukeley in 1724. Stukeley was the first to suggest that the stone circles and avenues of ancient Britain were huge serpent images

Below: a dragon-slaying carved on a pew-end in Crowcombe Church, Somerset

dragon, which is trying to bite his foot.

This alignment, though not straight enough to satisfy purists, marks an angle of astronomical significance. It takes in along its way Britain's largest prehistoric temple and its oldest Christian site. The dragon motif occurs a dozen times on the section running from St Michael's Mount to Avebury, enough for the image to be considered significant rather than coincidental. In the pantheon of British saints, Michael rates only fourth in popularity, but along this relatively short stretch of south-west England his name is invoked nine times.

The Book of Revelations (20:2) explains the significance of St Michael in this context:

And there was war in heaven; Michael and his angels fought against the dragon; and the dragon fought and his angels,
And prevailed not; neither was their place found any more in heaven.
And the great dragon was cast out, that old serpent, called the Devil, and Satan, which deceiveth the whole world: he was cast out into the earth, and his angels were cast out with him.

The form that the dragon took on earth is in question, but the earliest Christian missionaries evidently did not like whatever it was at all, and promptly set their own buildings on the ancient high places to banish the presence of the ancient spirit.

Christianity did not entirely eradicate the dragon, however, for church art did not always show it as the personification of evil – battered, spiked or trampled into extinction. There are dragons in churches all over the country – flying free, rampant on the tympanum of Penmon Priory in Anglesey, leering subversively at least nine times out of the 14th-century misericords in Wells Cathedral, twining unconquered round the enigmatic, disturbing doorway of Kilpeck Church in Hereford and Worcester. The authorities of course did not approve of these anarchic outbursts by their stone-masons and woodcarvers. 'What profit is there in these ridiculous monsters?' demanded Bernard of Clairvaux, founder of the Cistercian Order in the 12th century. 'For God's sake, if men are not ashamed of these follies, why at least do they not shrink from the expense?' Because, it seems, it was worthwhile keeping in with the old gods, just in case. . . .

Dragon ufonauts?

The nature of the worship that the dragon inspired is a question open to much speculative interpretation. One explanation identifies it with the UFO and sees the passage from Revelations as an account of some cosmic battle fought between the spaceships of warring galaxies. Indeed UFO sightings seem to cluster round dragon sites and along the ley lines, the dragon paths.

This theory suggests that Man, on first seeing the great discs, considered them to be sources of fabulous wealth. Inevitably, he coveted the possessions of the sky gods and tried to steal them, killing the gods, slaying the dragon, the guardian of treasure. Peredur in the *Mabinogion*, a collection of medieval Welsh tales,

heard how there was a serpent lying upon a ring of gold, without leaving a dwelling seven miles [10 kilometres] any side thereof. And Peredur went to where he heard the serpent was and he fought against the serpent with passion, valour and desperation and at last he slew it and took the ring for himself.

After the first appearance of the discs, the dragon/serpent, representing in its coils the circular UFO, became the object of a cult, and primitive Man constructed circular mounds and arrangements of stones, explicit only when seen from the air, to try to lure the flying saucers down to Earth again. Stonehenge, according to this theory, was built as a giant decoy.

This particular part of the theory is not new, for in the 18th century Dr William Stukeley had postulated that the circles and avenues of prehistoric Britain were huge representations of serpents that indicated some serpent- or dragon-worshipping religion that looked to the sky for its gods. He was howled down then with the same sort of derision that orthodox scholarship now pours on modern protagonists of the UFO school.

Accepting the link between dragons and UFOs, but radically reappraising the reasons for their tenacious but enigmatic position in our mythology, some original thinkers see both as psychic projections, manifestations conjured up either by some extra-terrestrial people of a higher order than Man, or by the collective unconscious. The scientist Thomas Bearden writes:

> The collective species unconscious is vastly more powerful than the personal unconscious and under appropriate conditions, it can directly materialize a thought form, which may be of an object, or even of a living being.

He calls the emerging thought form a *tulpa* and classes UFOs, fairies, Loch Ness monsters and other phenomena for which orthodox science has no explanation – including

Right: a detail from a Chinese plate of the early 18th century, showing a five-clawed imperial dragon. The imperial dragon symbolised power, and any commoner who dared use a dragon motif with five, rather than four, claws was immediately sentenced to death

Below: a mother-of-pearl inlay from a late 18th-century piece of furniture from Vietnam. It shows two dragons chasing a pearl, which is here portrayed as the interlocking symbol of *yin* and *yang*, the negative-feminine and positive-masculine forces in life

dragons – as tulpa materialisations.

A very different explanation links the dragon with some cosmic upheaval, an eclipse or a comet like the 'star of marvellous bigness', noted by Geoffrey of Monmouth in the 12th century 'spreading forth in the likeness of a dragon, and from the mouth of the dragon issued forth two rays, whereof the one was of such length that it did seem to reach beyond the regions of Gaul.'

A similar theory suggests that dragon legends all spring from a time when the orbit of Venus came close to the Earth with a ruinous effect upon Man's life here. Early Man was evidently much preoccupied with astronomy and the stars. Myths from the Aztecs, the Assyrians and Babylonians speak of Venus as 'the feathered serpent', 'the fearful dragon' that nearly destroyed the Earth with frightful fire and flood.

The difficulty in pinning down the dragon image lies in the fact that, to a great extent, it seems only to reflect the obsessions of those who pursue it. Modern psychology quite happily interprets it simultaneously as a father-figure guarding the treasure of his daughter's virginity and also, more tortuously, as a mother-figure, guardian of the capricious sexual drive of her son.

Alchemists of the Middle and Dark Ages accepted the dragon's mutability without concern, for their whole business centred on transmutation. For them, stability of form and function was already in question. Later, the practice of alchemy was made illegal and those who wrote about it did so in a code that used symbols to describe different forms of matter. The dragon was matter in its imperfect state; it was also identified with mercury, which could cause change in other metals. It guarded the hoard of gold that was the spur and inspiration for all the alchemists' work. The dragon had to be 'slain' to release the gold, but the slaying was also a fertilising, so that the dragon's death was also its rebirth in a different form.

It has appeared as the beginning of all things and the end of chaos, as fire breather and rain giver, earth force and sky god, life and death. The dragon image refracts into a thousand different notions, mirroring Man's obsessions through thousands of years. There is no conclusion to be drawn. All we can say is that the dragon is very old and that it is very strong.

The legend of lost Atlantis

A detailed description of Atlantis, a dazzling ancient civilisation swept away by a natural calamity, was set down as historical fact by the greatest of Greek philosophers. Today its location and very existence are hotly debated. RICHARD THOMAS surveys the arguments

MORE THAN 9000 YEARS before the birth of Christ, all North Africa west of Egypt and Europe from Spain to northern Italy lay under the imperial power of Atlantis, a continental state lying to the west of the Pillars of Heracles (the Straits of Gibraltar). Atlantis was peopled by the descendants of the sea-god Poseidon, who had coupled with a mortal woman. The island continent took its name from the giant Atlas, one of Poseidon's sons. The nation had prospered for many millennia. 'For many generations, as long as the divine nature lasted in them . . . they despised everything but virtue . . . but when the divine portion began to fade slowly' they became 'tainted with unrighteous ambition and power'.

The Atlanteans launched a war against the neighbouring areas of Europe and Asia. Resistance was led by the Greeks – specifically, by the early Athenians. And this may not be surprising, for the story was retailed by an Athenian – the philosopher Plato, writing in the fourth century BC. According to his account, the early Athens was pre-eminent in courage and military skill, and was the leader of the Hellenes. And when the rest fell off from her, being compelled to stand alone, after having undergone the very extremity of dangers, she defeated and triumphed over the invaders, and preserved from slavery those who were not yet subjugated, and generously liberated all the rest . . . who dwelt within the pillars. But afterwards there occurred violent earthquakes and floods; and

Right: Plato and his pupil Aristotle (far right), the first of many critics who have regarded Atlantis as Plato's invention

Below: the site of Atlantis, according to Ignatius Donnelly's theories of 1882. He claimed the light areas were colonised by the Atlanteans. Plato's account was very different (bottom left). He believed that the world known to him was encircled by the Atlantic, itself enclosed by a super-continent

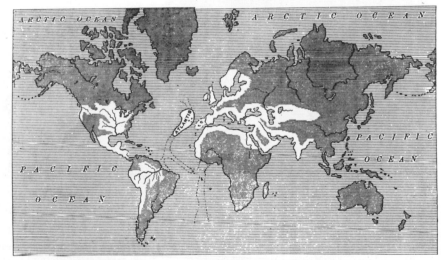

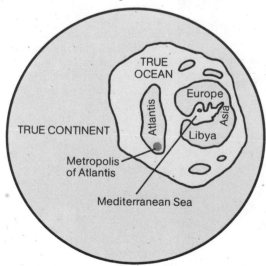

The statesman Solon is said to have been told of Atlantis while in Egypt in 600 BC

in a single day and night of misfortune all [the Athenians'] warlike men in a body sank into the earth, and the island of Atlantis in like manner disappeared in the depths of the sea . . . .

Plato says the story of Atlantis was brought back to Athens from Egypt by the sage and statesman Solon. Some time soon after 600 BC Solon had visited Saïs, capital of Lower Egypt and cultural centre of the civilised world. There the famous archives of ancient Egypt, dating back many thousands of years (and now also lost), were shown to him by Sonchis, the high priest of Egypt. These archives recounted the history of Atlantis.

Plato's narrative is the sole ancient source of the Atlantis legend. Yet the awe-inspiring scale of the drama – of a wealthy, powerful

Left: the god Atlas, condemned to hold the sky on his shoulders for ever. According to Greek myth, a daughter of Atlas lived on a western island. It may have been this that prompted Plato to give the name Atlas to the semi-divine first ruler of the island he described. He was one member of the eldest pair of twins fathered by the sea-god Poseidon on a mortal woman, Cleito

and corrupt continent, abruptly consumed by some great natural cataclysm – has gripped the Western imagination ever since.

Despite its flattering account of Athenian antiquity, even some of Plato's compatriots, including his great pupil Aristotle, cast doubt on the historical truth of the story. However, for centuries Atlantis was generally regarded as factual. Medieval sea charts often showed legendary islands in the Atlantic, generally supposed to be blessed with idyllic climates and ways of life. In the 15th century Portuguese maps showed Antilia, a mythical island whose name may have been derived from 'Atlantis'. It was reputed to have been the home of an ideal Christian society during the era of Moorish occupation of Spain and Portugal.

Academics debated the reality of Atlantis during the following centuries. But the modern popularisation of the legend dates back to 1882, when the American writer-politician Ignatius Donnelly published his *Atlantis: the antediluvian world*, placing Atlantis squarely on the Azores in mid-Atlantic. Bombarding the reader with a mass of loosely connected facts about the anthropology and mythology of peoples around the world, he attempted to prove that Atlantis

Left: part of the Royal Palace at Knossos, on Crete. The existence of an ancient maritime civilisation on this eastern Mediterranean island was unsuspected before the pioneering excavations of Sir Arthur Evans in 1900. Many orthodox archaeologists now regard the 'Minoan' civilisation as the most likely candidate for the historical origin of the Atlantis legend. The palace covered 5 acres (20,000 square metres) and had advanced plumbing and drainage. The downward-tapering pillar seen here is typical of Minoan architecture. The kilts of the servants carrying pitchers in the mural are also typical of the Minoans. Foreign envoys are depicted as similarly dressed in wall-paintings in Egypt, reputed source of the Atlantis legend

Right: the capital city of Atlantis, reconstructed according to the highly detailed description given by Plato. The god Poseidon had dug three circular canals, like moats, around a central hill. They were impassable, for 'at that time there were no ships and the art of sailing was then unknown'. Generations later the canals were spanned by bridges and linked by tunnels, each big enough for a single trireme (a galley with three banks of oars). Metal-clad walls enclosed the circles of land and an area beyond, 50 stadia across. This was probably about 6 miles (10 kilometres). The largest of the many temples on the central citadel was dedicated to Poseidon and Cleito, his human consort. The island was divided among 10 kings descended from Poseidon's 10 sons by Cleito. The royal palace was distinguished by its luxurious appointments, including hot and cold baths. Savage bulls were kept in its grounds. When the kings met to administer the law, they had first to capture one of the bulls and sacrifice it, allowing its blood to run over a pillar on which the laws were engraved

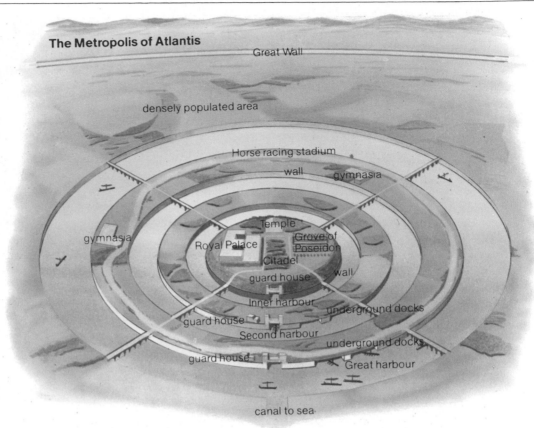

The Metropolis of Atlantis

Great Wall

densely populated area

Horse racing stadium

wall

gymnasia

gymnasia

Temple

Royal Palace

Grove of Poseidon

Citadel

guard house

wall

Inner harbour

underground docks

guard house

Second harbour

underground docks

guard house

Great harbour

canal to sea

was the ancient paradise of the world's myths, and that it had colonised the New World as well as the Old.

Atlantis became the subject of prolific speculation. Madame Helena Blavatsky, founder of the Theosophical Society, published *The secret doctrine*, embodying wisdom said to have been first set down in Atlantis in a forgotten language. She also disclosed the existence of several other continents, including Lemuria, which was to become a favourite with the pro-Atlanteans.

The Austrian Rudolf Steiner, founder of the Anthroposophical Society, further elaborated the story of the lost continents. He credited the Lemurians with the ability to lift weights by pure willpower, and the Atlanteans with mastery of the 'life force', with which they powered their aircraft.

The myth has continued to gather detail during the 20th century. Mu, located like Lemuria in the Pacific, was added by Colonel James Churchward, who claimed to have learned of it from ancient Indian inscriptions on stone tablets. Today, societies such as the Atlanteans and, in America, Atlantis Rising now flourish.

Orthodox archaeological study was also stimulated by the vogue of Atlantis. In an article in *The Times* in 1909, K. T. Frost suggested that Atlantis was in fact the Minoan civilisation, based on the island of Crete in the eastern Mediterranean. This was to become the most favoured theory of the academic establishment.

However, archaeological evidence supporting an Atlantic location for the lost continent was found in an unexpected area in 1968. Under the shallow waters of the Great Bahama Bank numerous stone slabs were found, perfectly jointed together, making up what has been dubbed the 'Bimini road'.

Was the ancient mystery finally solved? Had Atlantis been found? The newspapers certainly thought so, especially in America. But the bare fact of the matter is that, despite centuries of investigating, speculating and arguing, we are still none the wiser: the existence of Atlantis has been neither proved nor disproved.

But absence of proof is very different from disproof. And history is littered with 'mythical' cities and civilisations that archaeology

Right: Ignatius Donnelly, Congressman, scholar and novelist, who inspired the modern fascination with the legend of Atlantis

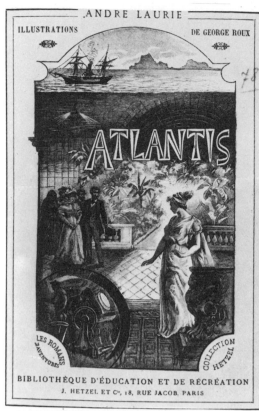

ANDRE LAURIE

ILLUSTRATIONS   DE GEORGE ROUX

ATLANTIS

LES ROMANS D'AVENTURES   COLLECTION HETZEL

BIBLIOTHÈQUE D'ÉDUCATION ET DE RÉCRÉATION

J. HETZEL ET Cⁱᵉ, 18, RUE JACOB, PARIS

Left: the Atlantis legend, revived in the late 19th century, inspired fiction as well as supposedly factual revelations. In this 1895 novel a party of explorers find Atlantis still flourishing on the seabed

Right: Rudolf Steiner, one of the mystics who claimed to have gained knowledge of Atlantis by psychic means

Below: the site of Troy. The city, besieged and sacked because of the abduction of the beautiful Helen, was long thought to be pure fiction. Heinrich Schliemann proved, in digs carried out from 1870 to 1890, that a real Troy existed and fell in about 1250 BC. These ruins, dating from a later Greek occupation, mark the site. Will a real civilisation be found to lie behind the legend of Atlantis?

has discovered to be fact. The discovery of Nineveh by Layard, of Troy by Schliemann and of the Minoan civilisation by Evans are cases in point.

And if Atlantis were to be found it could settle a controversy about Man's origins that has created a three-way split between what may roughly be described as 'rationalists', 'occultists' and 'fringe' scientists.

The rationalists insist that, in order to assert that Atlantis once existed, we need evidence that meets the usual scientific standards. The 'fringe' scientists would agree – but they have very different ideas about what the evidence is, and what it shows. The occultists say that Atlantis existed on the basis of intuition, inspiration, or communications from the 'other side'. It does not need any further proof. According to them, Atlantis was a civilisation that preceded ours and is the source of all 'magic' – the so-called ancient or secret wisdom behind the occult and mystery schools, linked to such relics of the past as Stonehenge, the pyramids of Egypt and the worldwide legends of giants.

If Atlantis is found, the occultists say, it will clearly show the falsity of the assumption on which conventional scholarship relies – that sophisticated human civilisation (at least as represented by city-dwelling) began 10,000 years ago at the outside, in Mesopotamia. It will mean that we are not the first 'super-race' on Earth, as we have hitherto thought – and may not even be the second, but simply the latest (many say the fourth or fifth) in a long line of civilisations going back anything from 65,000 to 650,000 years. And, they say, the lost civilisations are completely responsible for all the 'unexplained' phenomena around the world, from megaliths to magic. Lemuria and Mu are part of a coherent plan of cosmic evolution that takes in all time and all space. The physical discovery of Atlantis would herald the confirmation of that cosmic vision.

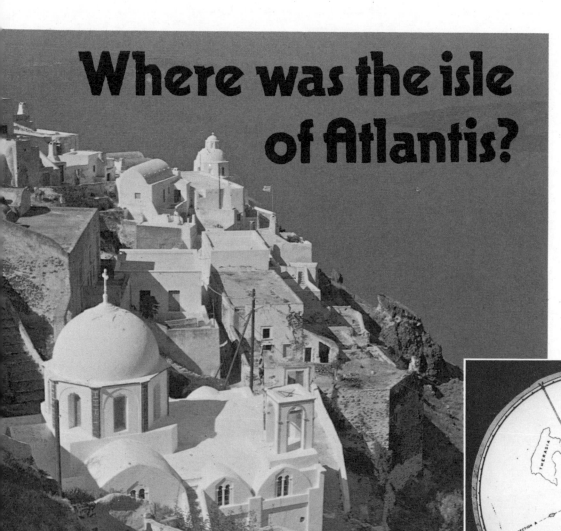

Where was the isle of Atlantis?

Left: Santorini, on Thera, the southernmost island of the Greek Cyclades group – and possibly the site of Atlantis

Below: a map by Greek scholar Dr Angelos Galanopoulos of the Thera group of islands. Dr Galanopoulos claims that the crater at the centre of the group was the site of Atlantis, destroyed in a volcanic eruption around 1500 BC

Bottom left: a vision of the delights of paradise before the Fall, by the Dutch artist Hieronymus Bosch (c.1450–c.1516). Many people believe that the true paradise was located on Atlantis

THE ISLAND OF SANTORIN
and
THE METROPOLIS OF ATLANTIS
AFTER PLATO (KRITIAS, 430 VBC)

Did the magical island of Atlantis ever really exist? Modern research suggests it may have done – though perhaps not in the Atlantic Ocean as Plato, originator of the myth, claimed

ATLANTIS: FACT OR FICTION? was the title of a symposium organised by the Department of Classical Studies at Indiana University in April 1975. Experts in various fields of learning, from classics to geology, came together to attempt to settle the Atlantis question once and for all. In many people's minds they succeeded – and proved Plato's 2300-year-old story to be mere fiction.

Yet the final words by Professor Edwin Ramage, editor of the subsequent book, were far from conclusive. 'No-one,' he writes, 'has yet offered a satisfactory solution to the problem – if, that is, there is a problem at all.' And, sure enough, new theories and new books continue to appear.

If Atlantis is a myth, it is one that will not disappear. It owes a great deal to Ignatius Donnelly's best-seller *Atlantis: the antediluvian world* (1882). At the start of the book, reprinted some 50 times before being revised in 1950, Donnelly listed what he called 'several distinct and novel propositions', summarising his extraordinary thesis:

1. That there once existed in the Atlantic Ocean, opposite the mouth of the Mediterranean Sea, a large island, which was the remnant of an Atlantic continent, and known to the ancient world as Atlantis.
2. That the description of this island given by Plato is not, as has long been supposed, fable, but veritable history.
3. That Atlantis was the region where man first rose from a state of barbarism to civilization.
4. That it became, in the course of the ages, a populous and mighty nation, from whose overflowings the shores of the Gulf of Mexico, the Mississippi river, the Amazon, the Pacific coast of South America, the Mediterranean, the west coast of Europe and Africa, the Baltic, the Black Sea, and the Caspian were populated by civilized nations.
5. That it was the true Antediluvian world; the Garden of Eden; the Gardens of the Hesperides; the Elysian

Fields; the Gardens of Alcinous; the Mesomphalos; the Mount Olympus of the Greeks; the Asgard, or Avalon, of the Eddas [medieval Icelandic poems]; the focus of the traditions of the ancient nations; representing a universal memory of a great land, where early mankind dwelt for ages in peace and happiness.

6. That the gods and goddesses of the ancient Greeks, the Phoenicians, the Hindus, and the Scandinavians were simply the kings, queens and heroes of Atlantis; and the acts attributed to them in mythology, a confused recollection of real historical events.

7. That the mythologies of Egypt and Peru represented the original religion of Atlantis, which was sun-worship.

8. That the oldest colony formed by the Atlanteans was probably in Egypt, whose civilization was a reproduction of that of the Atlantic island.

9. That the implements of the Bronze Age of Europe were derived from Atlantis. The Atlanteans were also the first manufacturers of iron.

10. That the Phoenician alphabet, parent of all the European alphabets, was derived from an Atlantis alphabet,

Above: the distinguished Greek archaeologist Professor Spyridon Marinatos inspecting ancient ruins on the island-volcano of Thera in the Greek Cyclades which, he believed, was the site of Atlantis

perplex mankind'. And Donnelly's 'brave new vision' is still the basis for the flood of books on Atlantis, from the occult to the 'rebel scientific', that continues to pour from the presses.

Donnelly's claims are often based on wrong or incomplete information, as scholars delight in pointing out. But their own claims are also often suspect; the moral for any would-be seeker after the truth of the Atlantis legend is to ignore both sides and to return directly to Plato's story. Even if it is full of distortions and literary devices for the purpose of propaganda or instruction, as some academics claim, it may yet hide a lost truth somewhere.

By this criterion, two recent hot favourites for the 'Atlantis found' title are suspect: an eastern Mediterranean civilisation, centred on Crete or Thera; and northern Europe, including Scandinavia.

Dr James Mavor's book *Voyage to Atlantis* caused a minor sensation in 1969. It set out the claims, first made by the Greek scientists Dr Angelos Galanopoulos and Professor Spyridon Marinatos, that Atlantis was in fact the Minoan civilisation, and that it was destroyed by the eruption of the island-volcano Thera about 1500 BC.

The name 'Minoan' was given to the

which was also conveyed from Atlantis to the Mayas of Central America.

11. That Atlantis was the original seat of the Aryan or Indo-European family of nations, as well as of the Semitic peoples, and possibly also of the Turanian races.

12. That Atlantis perished in a terrible convulsion of nature, in which the whole island was submerged by the ocean, with nearly all its inhabitants.

13. That a few persons escaped in ships and on rafts, and carried to the nations east and west the tidings of the appalling catastrophe, which has survived to our own time in the Flood and Deluge legends of the different nations of the Old and New Worlds.

What Donnelly had done was to take Plato's original 7000-word story and extend it to offer a whole new version of Man's prehistory and 'solve many problems which now

Many people, inspired by Ignatius Donnelly's classic study *Atlantis: the antediluvian world* (1882), believe that mankind first rose to a state of civilisation in Atlantis. They claim that the Sun-worship found throughout the world – for example in the Sun-motifs of the mysterious carvings of the Nazca plain (above left) and the cult of Ra, the Sun god of ancient Egypt (above) – are relics of the original religion of Atlantis. The Christian legend of the Flood, shown here in a Coptic manuscript from Ethiopia (right) is interpreted as a jumbled memory of the final submersion of Atlantis

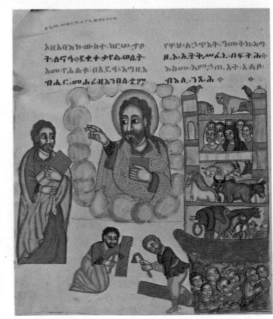

ancient civilisation of Crete by the British archaeologist Sir Arthur Evans, who began to excavate its remains in 1900. He believed that shadowy memories of it inspired the Greek myth of Minos, son of Zeus and king of Crete, who kept a bull-headed monster, the Minotaur, imprisoned in a labyrinth. At Knossos, Evans discovered the ruins of a splendid palace in which there was a bull-ring. In the reliefs and murals that adorned the palace, and in pictures painted on the large quantities of pottery that were found, there were representations of bull-hunting and bull-fights, conducted by youths armed only with staves and nooses.

In Atlantis there was also a cult of bulls, according to Plato: every four or five years the 10 kings of the island had to face the bulls unarmed, capture one and sacrifice it.

Death of paradise

By 1500 BC Crete was the centre of a powerful seafaring empire. Yet within an extraordinarily short time her power collapsed. There was widespread destruction of temples and other buildings throughout Crete, and the Minoan colonies and trading posts oversea were abandoned or destroyed; there was an abrupt change in artistic styles, and the quantity of pottery made sharply decreased; a large proportion of the Cretan population migrated to the west of the island; and soon political power in the Aegean shifted to Mycenae, on the Greek mainland.

Marinatos and Galanopoulos claimed that the eruption of Thera, known to have occurred about 1500 BC, could have caused this collapse. The tidal waves from the explosion, which must have been at least as powerful as that of Krakatoa in 1883, would have drowned many of the inhabitants of coastal towns throughout the Aegean, and the volcanic ash and dust that would have been deposited, in layers perhaps 20 inches (50 centimetres) thick, would have ruined harvests for years. Marinatos and Galanopoulos hold that Thera was actually the metropolis of Minoan civilisation, rather than being an outpost, as is generally believed.

The fall of Minoan civilisation was about 900 years before Solon received the story of Atlantis from the Egyptian priests, rather than the 9000 reported by Plato for the sinking of Atlantis. Crete was probably the country known to the Egyptians as Keftiu – a land with which they were in regular commercial and political contact, but that was for them in the 'far west', and was 'the way to other islands and the continent beyond' – as Plato described Atlantis.

The claim that Minoan civilisation was Atlantis is in many ways highly credible, and remains the most favoured by those few academics who still show any interest in the subject. Yet Mavor and his supporters have had to perform some deft twists of scholarship to prove their case.

Does the Minoan civilisation really match

Above: the German scholar Dr Jürgen Spanuth, who has made out a fairly convincing case for his claim that Atlantis was actually located, not in the Atlantic or Mediterranean, but on islands off the German coast

Plato's descriptions of Atlantis as closely as Mavor claims? An eloquent opponent of the claims for Crete or Thera is the German scholar Dr Jürgen Spanuth, who accuses its supporters of 'a gross logical error':

> Neither Thera nor Crete lies in the Atlantic . . . neither island lies at the mouth of a great river, neither was swallowed up by the sea and vanished.
> . . . In fact this great breakthrough in archaeology is a bubble that burst long ago.

Spanuth himself attempts to prove, in his 1976 book *Atlantis of the north*, that Atlantis was centred on the sunken islands near Heligoland, off the north-west German coast, and was in fact the Bronze Age forerunner of the Viking civilisation of northern Europe and Scandinavia, also known as Atland.

Spanuth, although presenting a highly convincing case, uses the same twists of scholarship that he so readily condemns in others – locating his version of the events in the North Sea instead of the Atlantic. Robert Scrutton does much the same thing in *The other Atlantis* and *The secrets of lost Atland*, also promoting the case for a proto-Viking Atlantis.

All these recent attempts to locate and

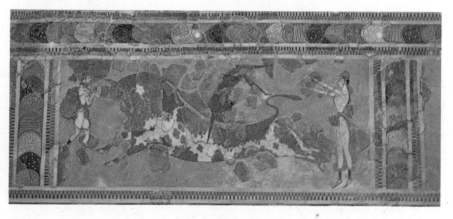

Above: a mural from the palace of Knossos on the island of Crete, depicting the ritual bull-leaping that was an integral part of Minoan culture. Plato, the originator of the Atlantis myth, wrote of a bull cult on Atlantis; this has led some experts to suggest that Atlantis was in fact the ancient civilisation of Crete

prove Atlantis deserve respect for their openness to the idea that Plato's legend is a story based on fact – but have then proceeded to alter the story to suit historical events at a different time in a different place.

Plato as adapted for consumption in the 20th century seems a far cry from the Plato of fourth-century Greece. It is fair to wonder if he would approve of the modern detective stories emerging from his tale. Would he think them nearer the truth or farther from it? A help or a hindrance in the search for the real origins and purpose of men?

Does, in fact, the real story still lie hidden where Plato quite specifically put it – on a huge land-mass to the west of Gibraltar, which disappeared beneath the sea nearly 12,000 years ago as the result of a colossal natural disaster?

If Atlantis did exist, what could have destroyed it? Where is the best place to look for its remains? There is no shortage of speculation seeking the answers to the mystery of a legend that refuses to die

THEORIES OF ATLANTIS that place the lost civilisation in the Atlantic need not be inconsistent with those others that locate it in the Mediterranean, northern Europe and many other sites around the world. For they could all be Atlantean: surviving colonies, which continued with similar cultures after the disaster that overtook the parent civilisation. The ancient societies of Crete, Sumeria, Egypt, Scandinavia, Britain the Azores, Brittany and the Basque country then become descendants of the lost empire.

The late T. C. Lethbridge, a Cambridge

A mountain peak of Atlantis, according to those who believe the Azores are the remains of the sunken continent. Pico, seen here, is one of the island group, which rises from a submarine plateau in the Atlantic

archaeologist and psychical researcher, highlighted the resemblances between the story of Atlantis and the other legends of lost lands, such as the Breton land of Ys, the Cornish Lyonesse, the Avalon of Arthurian legend, the Irish Tír na nOc and so on. He also pointed out the similarities between the styles of tools and ornaments of early civilisations in Europe and America.

Lethbridge believed that Atlantis may have been Tartessos (the biblical Tarshish), ruled in Celtic mythology by Lugh of the Silver Arm and allegedly having a written history, now lost, going back 6000 years before Christ. Tartessos lay between two rivers in southern Spain, just outside the Pillars of Heracles (the Straits of Gibraltar), just as Atlantis did in Plato's tale.

Plato says that the sea beyond the Pillars

The legend lives on

was impassable to shipping in his own day, because of the residual mud shoals left behind by the sinking of Atlantis. Lethbridge pointed out that shoals exist on both the Spanish and African coasts outside the Straits.

One of the most persuasive of Atlantis theorists was Otto Muck, a prolific engineer credited with the invention of the snorkel and 2000 other patents. In *The secret of Atlantis*, Muck presents several lines of evidence that suggest an Atlantic location for Atlantis and that converge on the ninth

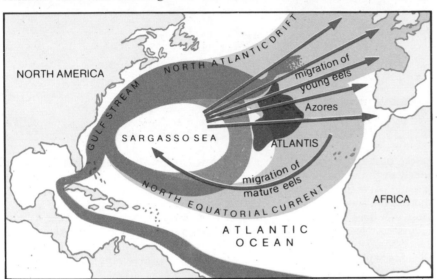

millennium BC as the date of some cataclysm that left its mark on the whole Earth.

The sinking of an ancient landmass in the Atlantic could explain the mysterious migrations of eels and birds. While migrating across the Atlantic, huge flocks of birds are often seen to circle for hours over an empty spot in the ocean before resuming their journey. It could be that this marks a place where once they would have found land.

The journey of the European eels across the Atlantic is an even greater puzzle. They

Below: in the present-day Atlantic the pattern of ocean currents (blue) aids the European eels in their gigantic migrations (arrows) to and from their spawning grounds in the Sargasso Sea. This mysterious behaviour may be a survival from a time when eels made a shorter journey to the rivers of Atlantis, using the ocean circulation of that era (grey)

Below: an asteroid is said by some theorists to have collided with the Earth in ancient times. Fiery debris rained on Atlantis, followed by tidal waves that inundated the island

Below right: this stone figure from Mexico shows an Atlantean soldier, according to Lewis Spence

spawn in the Sargasso Sea in the south-western part of the North Atlantic. Then the tiny larvae embark on a three-year swim eastward with the warm current of the Gulf Stream. When those that have survived the hazards of the journey reach European waters, they migrate upriver, reach sexual maturity, and return. Then they travel westward again. Now that they have reached their maximum growth and strength, the journey takes only four months. When they are back in the Sargasso Sea, they mate and produce offspring, which will soon make the journey to Europe for themselves.

It has been shown that eels need fresh water in which to reach sexual maturity. But why make this enormous journey?

Muck suggests that when Atlantis occupied the central Atlantic, it broke the motion of the Gulf Stream. The eastward journey was the direct route to fresh water for eels in those days, and the instinct has survived long after the extinction of Atlantis.

Bombardment from space
But what was the cataclysm that destroyed that hypothetical landmass?

Muck points to evidence of the impact of a colossal body with the Earth in the southwest Atlantic. Twin depressions, 23,000 feet (7 kilometres) deep, lie in the sea floor close to Puerto Rico. On the North American mainland to the west, a vast area around Charleston, South Carolina, shows the effects of a massive cosmic bombardment. Aerial photography first carried out in 1931 revealed 3000 shallow, eroded troughs, occupying part of an elliptical area that extends out over the Atlantic. Muck deduces that these were caused by the fragments of an enormous body falling to Earth from the north-west.

From the extent of the scarring on the Earth's surface, Muck calculated that the asteroid was 6 miles (10 kilometres) wide and hit the Earth with an explosive force of

30,000 megatonnes of nitroglycerine – the equivalent of 3000 medium-sized hydrogen bombs. The impact triggered the earth-quakes referred to in Plato's story, and split the Atlantic open along the line of the present-day mid-Atlantic Ridge, sinking a large part of central America to form the Gulf of Mexico and the Caribbean.

Furthermore, the Earth's Poles were shif-ted, and a new geological age abruptly began. The seasons became sharply differentiated for the first time. Muck does not explain how life anywhere on Earth was able to survive such a hammer-blow to the planet, but he describes the devastation that resulted in certain areas. Vast clouds of moisture, ash and noxious gases were carried to the north-east and south-west from the impact site. Over large areas animals and human beings were asphyxiated. Torrential rains followed, creating a deluge in many areas, giving rise to the legends of a great flood.

Siberia, which until then had enjoyed a cool, but not freezing, climate, was suddenly plunged into Arctic cold. The carcases of thousands of mammoths and woolly rhino-ceroses were preserved in frozen mud, many of them to be found in good condition thousands of years later.

One of the many surviving group mem-ories of the traumatic event, Muck believes, was its commemoration as the starting point of the Maya calendar. He accepts the calcu-lation of some scholars that this date was 5 June 8498 BC. On that day the Moon, Sun and Venus were in alignment – the kind of

Right: Celtic mythology had its own 'Atlantis', the 'Promised Land of Saints' in the western ocean. St Brendan supposedly visited it, in a voyage celebrated in an Irish narrative

Below: was Cro-Magnon man an Atlantean colonist?

Below: authors disagree widely as to the location and extent of Atlantis. The sites shown here are only some of those that have been suggested. Theories about the destruction of Atlantis are equally varied. The asteroid impact point shown is favoured by Otto Muck. Advocates of Atland suggest an Arctic site

astronomical event that was significant to the Mayas. Muck believes that this particular conjunction played a role in the worldwide catastrophe. It was the gravitational pull of the Moon and Venus that deflected the asteroid from its orbit as it was passing close to the Earth. Muck even estimates the time of impact – about 8 p.m. on the longitude where the asteroid struck.

Muck reaffirms Donnelly's ideas about the parallels to be found between the cus-toms and legends of the Old and New

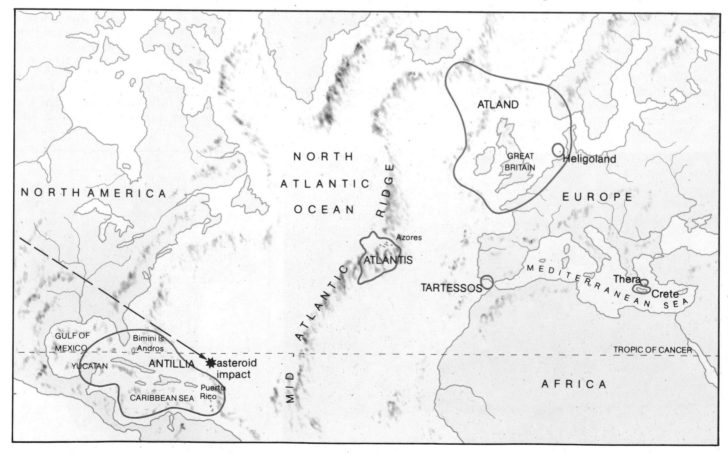

Worlds. He believes that the Atlanteans' immediate descendants, preserving their racial type, were the red-skinned American Indians and the Cro-Magnon people of Europe, who supplanted short, thick-set Neanderthal man. The Cro-Magnons were taller than Neanderthal man. Legends of giants and dwarves allegedly reflect their brief coexistence.

Another theorist who places Atlantis in the Atlantic is Maurice Chatelain, a French space engineer who worked with NASA on the Apollo missions. He refuses to believe that the eruption of Thera in 1500 BC could have been so catastrophic that it was able to bring down the Cretan civilisation and launch the Atlantis legend. Such an event would have been clearly recorded in the Bible, he says, and still remembered by the Greeks of 600 BC, when Solon heard the Atlantis story.

Chatelain accepts without qualms the claims of some writers that Phoenicians and even Hindus cultivated cotton and jute 2900 years ago in eastern Mexico, and that Sumerians and Phoenicians mined copper and tin in Peru and Bolivia 4300 years ago. But he claims that even these societies are too recent to be Atlantis. He agrees with Plato in placing the island civilisation at about 9000 BC. He bases this on the alleged evidence of an ancient scripture from – of all places – Tibet, which 'records that in 9564 BC a very

large part of the land sank into the ocean in what is now the Caribbean and the Gulf of Mexico.' And how did the Tibetans know about events in these distant places? Chatelain suggests that Atlantean refugees 'went all the way to Tibet to make sure they were on firm ground that wouldn't disappear beneath the waves again.' He continues:

It is easy to trace the east coast of the sunken Atlantis along the line drawn

The pyramid of Kukulcan at Chichén-Itzá in Yucatan, Mexico. The Mayan pyramids resemble the earliest, stepped pyramids of ancient Egypt, and are cited as evidence that Old and New World civilisations had a common origin – perhaps in Atlantis

An unshaken belief

Since interest in Atlantis was revived by Ignatius Donnelly in 1882, the subject has been enthusiastically espoused by occultists. The Russian-born Madame Blavatsky claimed to have written *The secret doctrine* under the guidance of the Mahatmas, spiritual masters dwelling in Tibet who communicated with her on the 'etheric plane'. Her account of Atlantis was expanded by her follower W. Scott-Elliot into an extraordinarily intricate history of early races, all unknown to science, of which the Atlanteans were only one. The first of a series of catastrophes was allegedly suffered by Atlantis 800,000 years ago. The last was in 9564 BC. Each of the Atlantean subraces gave rise to some modern human race. The story extends far into the future, when humanity will migrate to the planet Mercury.

Rudolf Steiner, another Theosophist, narrated his own history of Atlantis and other lost civilisations in *Cosmic memory*. His Atlanteans were unable to reason, but possessed mastery of magic. Reason appeared with the emergence of the Semites from the Atlanteans.

A Scottish occultist, Lewis Spence, who at one time was Chief Druid, wrote

Madame Blavatsky (above), Lewis Spence (below) and Alex Sanders (right) have all infused fresh life into the legend of Atlantis

Will Europe follow Atlantis? in 1942. He was not the last to read the world's future in the Atlantean past. He claimed that Europe would be subjected to floods, earthquakes and other natural disasters, owing to her corruption by the forces of Nazism and Fascism.

'Aquarian Age' speculation has been more optimistic. The belief in the ex-

istence and continuing influence of Atlantis is universal in occult circles. Typical are the firm Atlantean convictions of the British 'King of the witches', Alex Sanders. He claims that those now advanced in occult wisdom made progress in former lives, in Atlantis and other civilisations that, unlike our own, were nurtured by ancient esoteric knowledge.

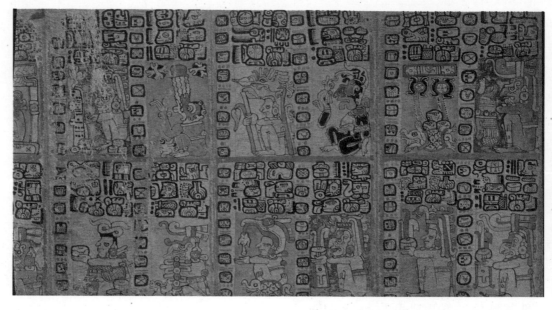

Right: this Mayan manuscript may contain an account of the destruction of much earlier civilisations. The picture-writing is vivid, but its meaning is obscure. An eminent French ethnographer, Brasseur de Bourbourg, claimed in 1869 to have deciphered this document. His translation tells of the annihilation, millennia before, of two countries that were rocked by great earth-tremors and 'suddenly disappeared in the night', along with 64 million people

from Florida to the Bahamas, Hispaniola, Puerto Rico, the Antilles, Trinidad, and the north coast of South America from the estuary of the Orinoco to that of the Amazon.

The final proof of this identification is provided, in Chatelain's view, by the underwater finds in the Bahamas. Off the island of Andros remains of an 'ancient temple' were found, measuring 75 feet by 90 feet (23 metres by 27 metres). There is considerable doubt about this, however, since an inhabitant of Nassau claims to have helped to build this structure in the 1930s, as a pen for sponges awaiting shipment. Chatelain seems unaware of this counter-evidence, as he makes no comment on it.

The Bimini road

Off North Bimini, Dimitri Rebikoff and J. Manson Valentine discovered a structure they called the 'Bimini road'. It was

an extensive pavement of rectangular and polygonal flat stones of varying size and thickness, obviously shaped and

Below: the underwater structure, J-shaped and apparently artificial, that has been named the 'Bimini road'. It has been suggested that when it was above water it was the lower part of a sea wall

accurately aligned to form a convincingly artifactual pattern. . . . Some were absolutely rectangular and some approaching perfect squares.

This feature is probably not a road, but later investigators still believe it to be a human construction, possibly a low wall.

Chatelain adds a detail to the evidence for a common source of at least some of the cultures on the two sides of the Atlantic. He tells of a missionary from the Basque country who travelled to Yucatan, home of the Aztecs, and before them of the Maya. He found he could make himself understood among the Indians by speaking his own native language. Basque is distinct from all other European languages, and its origin is still uncertain. Could the occurrence of a similar language on the other side of the Atlantic indicate a mid-Atlantic source?

Atlantis remains as mysterious as ever, and speculation continues to grow densely around it. Some believe that Atlantis has been found already – whether in the Aegean or in the Bahamas. Others await its imminent discovery on the slopes of the mid-Atlantic Ridge. Perhaps they will all be vindicated by the discovery of traces of a far-flung Atlantean empire in all these places.

The occultists have little interest in the discovery of tangible remains of Atlantis. They look forward, rather, to its resurgence: not a physical rising of the island, but a renaissance of 'Atlantean' virtues and powers. With the transition of the Earth from the Age of Pisces to the Age of Aquarius, they foresee the rediscovery of those mental and spiritual powers that they believe to have been the basis of Atlantean civilisation.

In the meantime the mystery remains to intrigue and tantalise us. Why is the Atlantis question so fascinating? Is it just that mankind has a need for such mysteries? Or do we all have a buried racial memory of a golden age in that once-fortunate land?

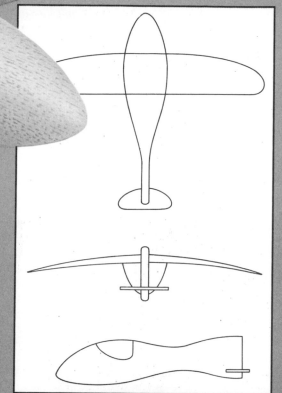

A catalogue of curious finds

Was Alessandro Volta really the first person to think of the electric battery? Were the Wright brothers really the first to fly? Modern research suggests that our ancient ancestors may have had technologies far more advanced than we can imagine, as CHRIS COOPER explains

IN A MUSEUM IN CAIRO a small wooden model was on display. No one could mistake what it was: one glance showed the wings, fin, tailplane and deep, bulky body of some kind of aircraft. The body of the model was just under 6 inches (15 centimetres) long, and its wingspan was just over 7 inches (18 centimetres). Made of light sycamore wood, it would glide a short distance when thrown from the hand.

It would not have been a great surprise to see a model like this in a science museum. But this model had pride of place as an exhibit in Cairo's Museum of Antiquities – and it was dated around 200 BC.

This ancient model is a glaring challenge to our ideas about the development of technology. And it is only one of innumerable oddities and enigmas that fuel speculation about the scientific knowledge and engineering skill of our ancestors.

No one had connected the model with the idea of artificial flight when it was found in 1898 – five years before the Wright brothers made their first successful powered flight – in a tomb in the ancient Egyptian city of Saqqara. It had been stored in a box with figurines of birds. It was not until 1969 that Dr Kahlil Messiha rediscovered it, and was astounded by its evident resemblance to a modern aircraft.

A committee of archaeological and aeronautical experts studied the model. They pointed out the cambering of its wings – the

Above: this working model glider was made in Egypt around 200 BC. Some experts believe it is a model of a full-sized 'powered glider'; others, however, have pointed out that it could be a weather-vane

Below: gold ornaments from South America, made some time between AD 500 and 800. One of them (left) bears a striking resemblance to a modern delta-winged jet

curve of the upper surface, which generates lift – and the 'anhedral' or downward droop of its wingtips, which provides stability. They conjectured that the craft was a model of a full-sized aircraft. It would have been a 'powered glider', designed to carry heavy loads at very low speeds – probably less than 60 miles per hour (95 km/h). It could have been propelled by an engine mounted at the rear, at a point where the model's tail is now broken.

The committee was sufficiently convinced of the importance of their find to devote a special display to it in Cairo. The discovery prompted a fresh look at 'bird models' in other collections. Over a dozen similar 'gliders' were found in other tombs. Could

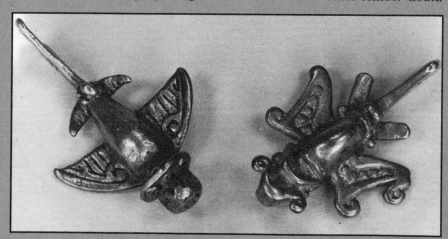

they really be models of ancient aircraft?

The scepticism that most people feel towards the idea of ancient aeronauts – possibly as shocking as that of ancient astronauts – receives a blow when it emerges that aero-modellers were apparently at work on the other side of the world during the first millennium after Christ.

The supposed aircraft models that have come to light are a number of small gold ornaments that have been found in Colombia, Costa Rica, Venezuela and Peru. One example was spotted in a collection of ancient art objects from Colombia by Ivan T. Sanderson, head of the Society for the Investigation of the Unexplained in the United States. It was a pendant 2 inches (5 centimetres) long, intended to be worn on a necklace or bracelet. The Colombian archaeologists

One of the most impressive pieces of evidence for the highly advanced states of some early technologies is the so-called 'Baghdad battery' (below). It was made during the Parthian occupation of Iraq at some time between 250 BC and AD 224 – and, astonishingly, could have been made to generate electricity. A West German Egyptologist, Dr Arne Eggebricht (below left), has proved, using a model, that the battery could have been used for electroplating small figures with gold (bottom)

had classified it as 'zoömorphic', or animal-shaped. But it looks much more like a delta-winged jet fighter than like any animal or bird. It has triangular appendages that look just like the wings of several types of modern supersonic aeroplane, a small straight tailplane, a tail fin – and there are even what appear to be insignia on one side of the fin. Yet the ornament is attributed to the Sinu, a pre-Incan society that flourished from about AD 500 to AD 800.

Being so very small, and made of solid gold, the model does not fly, but the resemblance to certain advanced aircraft built since the Second World War is remarkable. Aeronautical experts and biologists have compared these ancient ornaments with the forms of bats, sting rays and birds, and concluded that, in many of them, the features that seem to be artificial far outweigh those

that seem to be organic in nature.

These objects *look* like jets – but how safe a guide is that? The symbol on the Colombian ornament's 'tail fin' resembles the Semitic 'beth', or letter B. Some writers have jumped to the conclusion that the aircraft shown came from the Middle East.

Over-enthusiastic interpretation may lead some people to regard *all* extravagant claims for ancient objects with suspicion, but it becomes necessary to pay serious attention when a *functioning* device from an 'impossible' date is discovered. The Saqqara glider is one example; an equally impressive one is the 'Baghdad battery'.

Externally, the battery is a clay pot, just under 6 inches (15 centimetres) tall. It is stoppered with bitumen, in which is mounted a copper cylinder that runs down about 4 inches (10 centimetres) inside the pot. The cylinder is made from strips of copper soldered together, and it is closed with a copper cap. Inside the cylinder is an iron rod that has been heavily corroded, apparently by acid. The pot was found in Baghdad, and apparently dates from some time during the Parthian domination of this part of Iraq, which lasted from 250 BC to AD 224.

Ancient electricity

When the archaeologist Wilhelm König came across this item in a museum in Iraq in 1937, he immediately saw how it could be used to generate an electric voltage. Experiments made with modern replicas some years later confirmed that it could have served this purpose. To generate a voltage, it would be necessary to pour a suitable liquid into the cylinder. A large variety of fluids could have been used, including acetic acid or citric acid (the main constituents of vinegar and lemon juice respectively), or copper sulphate solution. This arrangement will generate between $1\frac{1}{2}$ and 2 volts between the copper and the iron cylinder and the iron rod. If a series of such cells were linked (forming a 'battery' in the proper sense of the word), the available voltage could be increased substantially.

The most likely use for electricity among the Parthians would have been electroplating. The art of gilding figurines dated back centuries before then. The battery could have been used to apply a voltage between a metal statuette and an ingot of gold while both were immersed in an electrolyte. Gold would have been transferred through the liquid to be deposited as a thin film on the figure's surface.

Similar clay pots have been found at other sites near Baghdad. They are a salutary reminder that our conceptions of mankind's historical development are often based as much on ignorance as on knowledge.

The ability to generate electrical current could have been hit on as an isolated discovery. Static electricity was known to the ancients: they knew that when amber (in Greek, *elektron*) was rubbed, it would attract

light objects such as dust and hairs. The technique of generating electrical current – which is electric charge in motion – could have been an equally haphazard, isolated discovery. Neither finding seemed to lead to further technological development or insight into the causes of the phenomena, although some enthusiasts have claimed that the Parthians – and, before them, the ancient Egyptians – used electric light.

There are, however, enough soberly accredited anomalies of technology from the past to keep us well aware that some of our ancestors did develop their technology – to astonishingly high levels.

In 1900, sponge divers found the wreck of a treasure ship, almost 2000 years old, off the Greek island of Antikythera. It was laden with bronze and marble statues, and may have been voyaging to Rome when it went down in about 65 BC. In its cargo was found a mass of wood and bronze, the metal so badly corroded that it could only just be made out as the remains of gearwheels and engraved scales. It was not until 1954 that Derek J. de Solla Price of Cambridge University was finally able to deduce that here was an ancient analogue computing device, far ahead of anything that was to be seen in Europe again for hundreds of years. In fact the mechanism, when new, 'must have borne a remarkable resemblance to a good modern mechanical clock.'

The device consisted of at least 20 gearwheels, supported on a number of bronze plates, the whole mounted in a wooden box. When a shaft that passed through the side of the box was turned, the pointers moved at different speeds over dials, which were protected by doors. The inscriptions explained how to operate the machine and how to read the dials.

The device was a working model of the celestial bodies – Sun, Moon, and the planets that can be seen with the naked eye, Mercury, Venus, Mars, Jupiter and Saturn. Their relative positions in the sky were shown with great accuracy. The time of day

Among the treasures recovered in 1900 from a ship wrecked almost 2000 years ago off the Greek island of Antikythera was a confused mass of wood and bronze (above), so badly corroded that it was almost impossible to make out what it was. It was not until 1954 that a Cambridge scholar realised its true significance – the object consisted of more than 20 gearwheels mounted on a wooden box, and constituted a working model of the movement of the celestial bodies. Nothing so complex would be seen again until the clocks of the Renaissance, such as this one, made in Germany in the 15th century (right)

was also indicated by the pointers.

In Price's words, 'Nothing like this instrument is preserved elsewhere. Nothing comparable to it is known from any scientific text or literary allusion.' He goes on to say that 'it seems likely that the Antikythera tradition was part of a large corpus of knowledge that has since been lost to us but was known to the Arabs.' For mechanical calendar devices were made by them centuries later, and inspired the clock makers of medieval Europe.

But what else might such a body of knowledge have contained? What forces, benevolent or malevolent, might the ancients have commanded – that did *not* stay alive in the memory of their descendants?

Puzzles from the past

Did the Indians of South America use bulldozers to build their great cities? Did the ancient Egyptians invent television? Or are we in danger of seeing the past through modern eyes?

THE BELIEF THAT A SUPERB technological prowess was possessed by past civilisations, a prowess that is totally unacknowledged in the standard history books, is nourished by the oddities and anomalies that crop up here and there in galleries and museums. Often they have been shown for years as quite ordinary objects; and it takes a giant leap of the imagination to see them as anything else.

One of the ancient artefacts that has been reinterpreted by recent authors is a small figurine that was classified as a model jaguar when it was found in Panama in the 1920s. But it takes on a new appearance in the light of the suggestion that it was actually an earth-moving machine, like a present-day bulldozer. Despite the model's antiquity, the curious triangular appendages begin to look like shovels carried on mechanical arms. The cogged wheels that are mounted on the model's tail look as if they should engage with chains or belts. On the other hand, sceptics point out, the construction of a full-sized earth-mover would demand considerable technological resources – facilities for smelting iron, for example, and manufacturing large machine parts – of a kind for which

This golden figurine (below) was identified as a model jaguar in the 1920s. But some scholars have suggested that it is a model of an enormous bulldozer – the legs could be shovels, and the wheels on the tail look as if they could engage with a drive chain. Perhaps machines such as these were used to build the 'lost' city of Machu Picchu (bottom)

absolutely no evidence has been found.

The authors who discuss this curiosity are not slow to connect it with such prodigious feats of city-building as that represented by the 'lost' city of Machu Picchu, built 6850 feet (2100 metres) above sea level in the Peruvian Andes. They claim that machinery would have been needed to move the vast amounts of earth and stone required by the construction. But even this claim has little substance: it is quite possible that these huge feats demanded no more than muscle-power.

An even wilder identification is made in

deciphering a wall engraving in the Egyptian temple at Daendara, dating from between 300 BC and 30 BC, and dedicated to the goddess Hathor. According to American journalist Rene Noorbergen, a 'box' in the picture carries an image of the head of Horus, sun-god and symbol of divine energy. The head carries a sun-disc, which 'identifies the box as the energy source'. An electrical 'cable' runs from this to two objects that, Noorbergen alleges, are cathode ray tubes – devices that, it has hitherto been believed, were invented in the late 19th century and are the forerunners of the television tube. A cathode ray tube contains a vacuum, and, when it is operating, a stream of electrons flows along it from a heated cathode, or negative electrical terminal, to an anode, or positive terminal in the form of a fluorescent screen at the far end of the tube. Noorbergen claims that the 'cable' in the wall engraving runs to a cathode in each of the supposed tubes. In each tube a serpent extending from each cathode represents the stream of electrons. (He does not appear to see an anode, or positive terminal, which would be essential in such a tube.)

The baboon and the knife

One of the serpents lies straight along the length of the tube. The head of the other serpent is bent to one side – away from the figure of a baboon holding a knife. Noorbergen claims that this shows an electron beam being deflected by an electrically charged object – the knife. A demonstration of the properties of electrons is being portrayed.

The serpents symbolise electron beams, the sun-disc symbolises an electrical generator – what does the baboon symbolise? Noorbergen becomes literal-minded here and decides that a real baboon had been trained to carry out the experiment: 'the Egyptians were well aware of the powerful energies they were dealing with and took no chances by participating directly in the experiment themselves.'

Noorbergen's account seems, to many people, a little far-fetched. The astronomer Carl Sagan makes fun of the pastime of finding engineers' blueprints in works of art

The 'rustless' iron pillar at Meharauli, India, has given rise to a flight of fancy in the mind of Erich von Däniken that deserves to be quoted at length:

'In the courtyard of a temple in Delhi, India, there exists . . . a column made of welded iron parts that has been exposed to weathering for more than 4,000 years without showing a trace of rust for it contains neither sulphur nor phosphorus. Here we have an unknown alloy from antiquity staring us in the face. Perhaps the column was cast by a group of far-sighted engineers who did not have the resources for a colossal building, but wanted to bequeath to posterity a visible, time-defying monument. . . .'

It is only fair to say that von Däniken has since stated that he was misled by the column. This is hardly surprising; the above account misses some important points. The pillar is, in fact, made out of a single piece of pure iron – not several pieces of some mysterious alloy, welded together. Erected in the fifth century AD, the column weighs over 6 tonnes; what is remarkable is that not until the late 19th century could a single casting of a similar size have been made in Europe.

Below: figures from the Gate of the Sun, Tiahuanaco, high in the Bolivian Andes. Author Charles Berlitz claims that experts have seen in these designs evidence that the technology of the pre-Columbian people that built the temple was astonishingly advanced. The eye motif of the figure on the left looks like 'a jet-propelled vehicle', while that of the figure on the right resembles 'a deep sea diver or an astronaut'. But these observations, interesting as they are, hardly constitute hard evidence for his claims

that are normally regarded as having merely ceremonial or religious significance. He has found what looks like an amphibious vehicle in the carvings of the Temple of the Sun at San Juan Teotihuacan in Mexico. But he does not for a moment believe that it is anything other than the rain god, as the archaeologists say it is. It is not that an amphibious vehicle would be too exotic to be found in that society – it is that it is too prosaic, too similar to vehicles that happen to be current in our own century. Such interpretations are suspect because they make the people of the past too similar to ourselves. Sagan says, aptly: 'These artifacts are, in fact, psychological projective tests. People can see in them what they wish.'

It is salutary to be reminded of how mysterious the ways of alien cultures are – of the immense importance attached to activities that we cannot explain, and the huge labour expended on them. Striking examples are to be found littering the floor of the forests of Costa Rica.

When the Diquís Delta was being cleared for plantations in the 1930s, the workers found their task hindered by hundreds of stones that appeared to have been artificially smoothed, scattered over the forest floor. The largest were about 8 feet (2.5 metres) in diameter, and were nearly perfect spheres.

The stones were probably roughly shaped as they were hewn from natural blocks and then polished with smaller stones, with wet sand as an abrasive medium. Their shape must have been frequently checked with

accurate cut-out templates. The whole process must have required the patient labour of huge numbers of people over a long period.

Then the stones, some weighing as much as 16 tonnes, had to be dragged from the place where they were quarried, possibly at the mouth of the Diquís River, to their final resting places, perhaps 30 miles (48 kilometres) distant. They were often placed in groups, or in straight or curved lines. Some are to be found over human graves. But the purpose of this enormous effort is quite unknown. Some people speculate that the stones represent the Sun and Moon (and it has been suggested that they represent other heavenly bodies as well); others think they are intended as a physical embodiment of perfection. The two ideas may not be distinct if the makers of the stones viewed the heavenly bodies as perfect, as some ancient Greek philosophers did.

Conflicting clues

There is no technique for determining the date at which the stones were shaped. Remains associated with some particular ball

Above: part of the tiered base of the monumental temple of Quetzalcoatl at Teotihuacan, near present-day Mexico City. The carved heads are those of Tlaloc, the rain god, whose staring eyes signify far-sightedness, and Quetzalcoatl. The astronomer Carl Sagan has poked gentle fun at the over-enthusiastic interpretation of early images by pointing out that the head of Tlaloc looks rather like an amphibious vehicle. People tend to see, he says, what they wish

Below: Dr and Mrs Samuel Lothrop with one of the huge stone spheres they found in the jungles of Costa Rica in the 1940s. Many of the balls were as much as 8 feet (2.4 metres) in diameter. Who carved them, and why?

Scotland's unique vitrified forts are scattered from the Solway Firth up to the central Western Highlands and then across to Aberdeenshire, with a number along the north-west coastline and a few in the Western Islands. They are Iron-Age hilltop constructions, roughly circular in shape with walls ranging in height from 12 to 20 feet (4 to 7 metres) and they usually contain a shallow well, probably used for catching rainwater, in the centre. The walls are made of piled stones; but at some stage the rocks were subjected to intense heat and melted, flowing together to form a glassy, 'vitrified' mass. The degree to which the walls are vitrified varies from fort to fort.

The earliest antiquarians to study the forts, in the 18th century, suggested they had been built from volcanic rocks, but this is now known to be incorrect. The walls were fired *after* they were built. But it is not clear whether the firing was accidental or deliberate.

Many students of the forts are convinced that the walls were intentionally fired, either to strengthen them or to make them impervious to moisture. Only the most deliberate action, they believe, could achieve the searing temperatures – up to 2000°F (1000°C) – to which the rocks have, at some time, been exposed. But, they think, the enthusiasm of the builders must occasionally have overreached itself, since sometimes the walls have collapsed.

There has, of course, been specu-

occasionally give clues, but on the whole these conflict. So we do not know who the makers of the strange spheres were, nor what the aim of their activity was.

Infinitely patient grinding was also required to sculpt the superb features of the life-size quartz skull found in British Honduras in 1927 by the British explorer F. A. Mitchell-Hedges. He describes it:

The Skull of Doom is made of pure rock crystal and according to scientists must have taken 150 years, generation after generation working all the days of their lives, rubbing down with sand an immense block of rock crystal until the perfect skull emerged. . . . It is said that when he [the high priest of the Maya] willed death with the help of the skull, death invariably followed. It has been described as the embodiment of all evil.

Many of these assertions are perhaps the invention of Mitchell-Hedges himself. It has even been conjectured that he may have had the Skull of Doom made as a birthday present for his daughter. It was she who found it beneath the altar in the Mayan city of Lubaantum during excavations by

A burnt out case

lation that the vitrifying agency was actually some devastating heat ray wielded by alien beings against whom the fort-builders were defenceless. However, this exciting hypothesis has been invalidated by some recent research.

Experiments have convinced Ian Rawlston of the Department of Geography, Aberdeen University, that the vitrification of the hill forts is due to

The vitrified fort on Tap O'Noth in Aberdeenshire. According to an ancient Scottish ballad, it was the home of a giant named Jock or John O'Noth who, together with a friend who lived at the vitrified fort on the neighbouring mountain of Bannachie, fought the English

destructive acts, although sometimes it could have been accidental. Early in 1980 Mr Rawlston and a team from the university built a section of rampart after the fashion of the Pictish forts – laced together with seasoned timber, on top of a windy hill. He then piled wood against it and set fire to it, keeping the conflagration going for some days. And afterwards he found, in the heart of the wall, vitrified stone. 'The mass of evidence,' he says, 'points to the fact that vitrification was not a constructive process, and that the ramparts were probably fired by enemies, possibly Vikings, many years after they were constructed.'

But this may not be the final answer. Alexander Brown, a potter and kiln-builder, has experimented with firing the glacial boulder clay that is found all over Scotland. This vitrifies at a relatively low temperature – around 1000°F (550°C) – and, says Mr Brown, 'once vitrified, it resembles granite, and it is at least possible that the ancient Picts might use it as a facing material.'

But whatever the answer, one other mystery remains about the strange forts. Exactly similar edifices, of a similar age and built by people at a similar stage of technological advancement, are found in Germany, Scandinavia and Ireland, among other places. Most of them suffered attack during their occupied lives, but none shows traces of vitrification: why is it that Scotland's forts are unique in this way?

This extraordinary life-size quartz skull (left) was found in British Honduras in 1927. Only one other similar skull exists: also from pre-Columbian central America, it is now in the London Museum of Mankind. Quartz masks are, however, fairly common. Above is one that was made in Tibet

Mitchell-Hedges, on her 17th birthday.

Some of the detailing of the skull is considered to be astonishingly modern and naturalistic. To have ground such lovingly modelled objects from quartz, an extremely hard substance, would indeed have been a labour of devotion – unless the Maya had techniques available to them that we are not aware they possessed. Indeed, it is often suggested that ancient stonemasons must have had more effective cutting instruments available to them than the relics that have been found suggest, and perhaps even stone-softening liquids, in order to shape the intricately interlocking stones of such cities as Sacsahuaman in Peru. So perhaps sculptors working on a smaller scale were not, after all, condemned to the years of polishing of which Mitchell-Hedges wrote.

The function of the crystal skulls is not known. It has been suggested that they could have acted as centrepieces in some awe-inspiring temple ritual. But such explanations merely cloak our ignorance of the motivation of the ancient craftsmen.

Inadmissible evidence

Did men walk – and work – amid the primeval forests that we dig up as coal? Did men hunt the dinosaurs? Conventional historians say no – but striking evidence exists for such startling claims

ABOUT 1880 A COLORADO RANCHER went on a journey to fetch coal from a seam driven into a hillside. The particular load that he collected was mined about 150 feet (45 metres) from the mouth of the seam, and about 300 feet (90 metres) below the surface. When he returned home, the rancher found the coal lumps were too big to burn on his stove. He split some of them – and out of one of the lumps fell an iron thimble.

At least, it looked like a thimble – and 'Eve's thimble' was the name given to the object in the locality, where it became well-known. It had the indentations that modern thimbles have, and a slight raised 'shoulder' at the base. The metal crumbled easily, and flaked away with repeated handling by curious neighbours. Eventually it was lost. The author who described it in *The American Antiquarian* of 1883 asks:

Where did the thimble come from? How did it get there? Were there any of these western tribes who possessed such a thing before the coming of the white man?

But even if American Indians used similar iron 'thimbles' in past centuries, the mystery will not go away. For the coal from which the object came was formed between the Cretaceous and Tertiary periods, about 70 million years ago. And according to all received opinion, mankind did not exist at that date:

Above: a model from Dr Abner Weisman's collection of pre-Inca artefacts that, he claims, shows a woman who has undergone a Caesarian section. If true, this would indicate a very high level of medical skill in a 'primitive' culture – but a chilling alternative is that the model shows the victim of a particularly gruesome form of human sacrifice

Below: Rene Noorbergen, a leading proponent of a lost high technology

the nearest things to human beings were tiny lemur-like tree-dwelling mammals. Human intelligence had not appeared – let alone human technology capable of making and shaping iron.

Yet the 'thimble' fitted snugly into a cavity in the coal. What was happening on the Earth 70 million years ago, when this artefact was apparently made – and dropped?

Another out-of-place artefact made of iron was the subject of careful and detailed investigation in 1844. A block of stone 2 feet (60 centimetres) long, cut from Kingoodie quarry near Dundee in Scotland, was being cleared of the layer of soft clayey 'till' clinging to it. (The stone in the quarry occurred in layers alternating with layers of till.) A rusted iron nail was found where the stone and the till met. A half-inch (1.2 centimetres) of the nail at the pointed end projected into the till, while the rest lay along the surface of the stone – except for the final inch (2.5 centimetres) at the head end, which projected into the stone. It was not possible to tell which part of the quarry the block had been taken from, but it was estimated that the rock containing the nail had been formed 60 million years ago, a period that dwarfs the few millennia that human beings are known to have been smelting iron ore in Scotland.

Occasionally *objets d'art* have been found imprisoned in coal or solid rock. In 1852 a mass of rock was dynamited at Dorchester, Massachusetts, USA. Among the rock fragments workers found two fragments of a metal object. When put together they formed a bell-shaped vessel, $4\frac{1}{2}$ inches (11 centimetres) high and $6\frac{1}{2}$ inches (16 centimetres) across at the base. It seemed to be made of an alloy containing silver. On the sides there were, according to a contemporary report in *Scientific American*,

> Six figures of a flower, or bouquet, beautifully inlaid with pure silver, and around the lower part of the vessel a vine, or wreath, inlaid also with silver. The chasing, carving, and inlaying are exquisitely done by the art of some cunning workman. This curious and unknown vessel was blown out of the solid pudding stone, 15 feet [4.5 metres] below the surface . . .

The writer Rene Noorbergen reports cases in which gold artefacts have been found in 'impossible' places. Mrs S. W. Culp of Illinois was shovelling coal when a lump broke to reveal a gold chain, lying in a loop-shaped cavity within the lump. This was in 1891; nearly half a century before, in an English quarry, workmen blasting rock discovered a gold thread, later judged to be artificial, that had been embedded in granite several million years old.

One of the most famous out-of-place objects is known as the Salzburg cube. In 1885 a workman at an iron foundry in Austria was smashing chunks of coal from Wolfsegg

when he came across a roughly cubical iron object. Noorbergen repeats the description of the object that became current:

> The edges of this strange cube were perfectly straight and sharp; four of its sides were flat, while the two remaining sides, opposite each other, were convex. A rather deep groove had been cut all the way around the cube about midway up its height . . . Unfortunately the cube disappeared from the Salzburg Museum in 1910 . . .

In fact the 'cube' was probably never at Salzburg; for a while it was in a museum in Linz, and today it is in a local museum near the foundry where it was discovered. It is very far from being a cube: its only flat surface is the result of a slice being taken from it for chemical analysis. The analysis showed that the metal is free of nickel, chromium or cobalt, and therefore cannot be a meteorite – an early conjecture as to its origin. It seems to be a form of wrought iron.

It is not surprising that a wrought-iron artefact should be found lying on the floor of an iron foundry – even though the purpose of the object is unknown. The crucial question

New relics for old

Dr Janvier Cabrera Darquea of Ica, Peru, has been known to claim that the carvings on the stones in his huge collection show highly complex medical operations being carried out thousands of years ago (left, above). The stones have also been hauled into the ancient astronaut controversy by the irrepressible Erich von Däniken as, besides scenes of heart transplants and brain surgery, they depict astronomers gazing through telescopes and so on.

In fact the stones are made by a local artisan – whose name, according to the BBC television team who found him, is Basilio – and are blackened with boot polish before being fired in donkey dung (left, below) to give an impression of age. While there certainly is evidence that the ancient Peruvians were highly sophisticated, it does not appear that they were as advanced as the Ica stones pretend – nor that extra-terrestrials imparted any knowledge to them.

Left: artist's impression of letters, apparently deliberately carved, that were found on a block of marble taken from some 60 feet (18 metres) below ground near Norriston, Pennsylvania, USA. Were they made by the hand of Man – or is this a sly example of the cosmic joke?

is whether it really originated inside a chunk of coal. The scientist who first investigated the 'cube' and suggested that it was a meteorite apparently did not try to find the piece of coal with the cavity that was supposed to have contained the cube. So this most vital of clues was never preserved, and the reputation of the 'Salzburg cube' was blown up out of all proportion to its intrinsic interest. The case is an excellent illustration of the importance of the original eyewitness testimony concerning the discovery and of an immediate on-the-spot inspection.

There are many other accounts of items discovered in unexpected places. In 1967 human bones were reported to have been discovered in a vein of silver in a Colorado mine. A copper arrowhead 4 inches (10 centimetres) long accompanied them. The silver deposit was, of course, several million years old and much more ancient than humanity, according to generally accepted ideas.

The Creation Research Society, founded in the United States, works from religious conviction to overthrow the conventional wisdom about the evolution of species and searches for just such disturbing anomalies as those discussed above. In 1976 their journal published a description of a spoon found in 'soft Pennsylvania coal' in 1937.

The spoon was found in a mass of off-brown coloured ash which remained after burning a large piece of coal. The ashes, when disturbed, fell apart, revealing the spoon . . . This might well be a relic from the antediluvian world. The same conclusion might be drawn from a

slightly different kind of ancient 'artefact' – an extremely ancient specimen of what appears to be writing, described in the *American Journal of Science* of 1831. A block of marble taken from the earth at a depth of at least 60 feet (18 metres) was cut into slabs. One of the cuts exposed an indentation about $1\frac{1}{2}$ inches by $\frac{5}{8}$ inch (4 centimetres by 1.5 centimetres). In this shallow space were two raised forms resembling the letters I and U. The regularity of the letters gives every impression of two characters carved by human agency, and somehow preserved over the millions of years during which the marble formed – while all trace of the edifice on which they were carved, or of all associated carvings, was presumably wiped out.

Yet another type of 'artefact' is perhaps the most characteristically human of all – evidence of injury inflicted by one human being on another thousands of years old, yet performed with modern ingenuity.

The evidence is a skull now in the Natural History Museum in London. It belongs to a human being of the Neanderthal type, and was found near Broken Hill, in what was then Rhodesia and subsequently became Zambia, in 1921. On the left side of the skull there is a smooth round hole. The cleanness of the injury suggests that a high-speed projectile – a bullet – caused it. Directly opposite this wound, the skull is shattered, as by the projectile leaving the skull.

A Berlin forensic expert judged the hole to be like the bullet wounds with which members of his profession have to deal so frequently today. Yet the remains were found 60 feet (18 metres) below the surface. They could not have been covered to that depth by natural geological processes if the victim had died in the last few centuries, when firearms were first brought to Central Africa.

This puzzling object is not unique. The skull of an aurochs, an extinct species of bison, that was found near the Lena River in the USSR has a smooth, well-rounded hole, resembling a bullet wound. The aurochs lived for years after receiving this wound.

These skulls suggest the startling possibility that humankind's aggressiveness had

Above left: this skull found in Soviet Armenia is over 4000 years old – yet surgeons had plugged the hole in it with a piece of animal bone

Above: Professor Andronik Jagharian, who commented that the ancient surgeons were apparently technically superior to modern doctors

This Neanderthal skull has a small hole on one side (below) so clean that it looks like a bullet wound. And the damage on the other side (right) is indeed consistent with the effect of a high-speed projectile rather than that of a spear or arrow

more sophisticated instruments than flint axes at its disposal millennia ago. But healing skills may have been correspondingly developed also. We know little of prehistoric medicine: what we do know is almost wholly confined to the traces of surgical operations affecting bone. And these seem to show that brain surgery and even open-heart surgery were carried out more than 4000 years ago.

Near Lake Sevan, in Soviet Armenia, skeletons predating 2000 BC, from a people called the Khurits, have been found. In one of the women's skulls, a hole about $\frac{1}{4}$ inch (6 millimetres) had been made by some injury during life. The ancient surgeons had inserted a small plug of animal bone. It stayed in place, and the woman survived as her skull bone partially grew around it.

In another Khurit skull, a larger wound had been caused by some blow. Surgeons cut out an area of the skull around the wound in order to remove splinters from the brain. This patient, too, survived.

Professor Andronik Jagharian, who

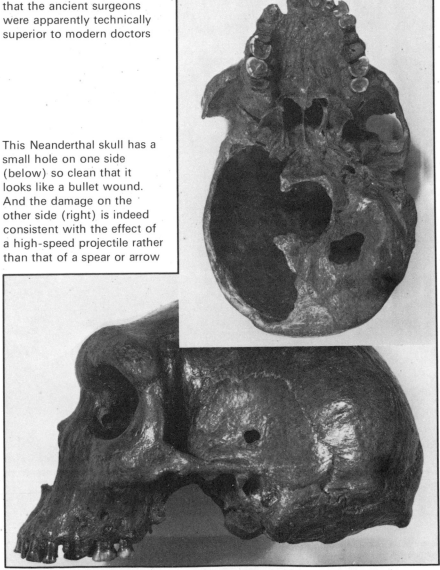

studied the skulls, commented: 'Considering the ancient tools the doctors had to work with, I would say they were *technically superior* to modern-day surgeons.'

Ancient skeletons from Central Asia studied at the University of Ashkhabad displayed traces of skull surgery and also surgery on the ribs. They strongly suggested that the heart had been exposed for surgical treatment.

Rene Noorbergen, who cites these cases, believes they show that the early people concerned were in contact with technically more developed cultures. They either learned to carry out these surgical practices themselves, or relied on 'missionaries' to do the work. He believes that the cultures from which the skeletons come could not have developed the techniques themselves.

He goes on to describe stone figurines and carvings found high in the Andes and long predating the Incas. Some of the carvings depict the victims of disease and bear the signs of smallpox, cancer or arthritis. These may have been instructional models, or may have been buried with actual victims for ritual purposes.

Unarguable evidence of the ancient super-races who were the supposed sources of prehistoric surgical skills is lacking in the archaeological record. But this is not necessarily damning. It is often pointed out that the entire fossil evidence on which the descent of Man from ape-like ancestors is so confidently based could easily be assembled in one large room. A very few new finds would be sufficient to shake the whole edifice. The Creation Research Society, in its attempts to do exactly that, displays some fossil footprints that completely contradict the orthodox view. Dinosaurs are supposed to have become extinct about 70 million years ago, whereas Man arose about a million years ago – despite those strip cartoons that show cavemen hunting, or being hunted by, the giant reptiles. Yet in the bed of the

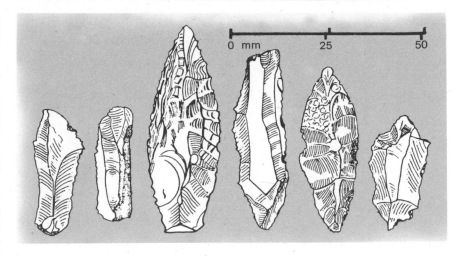

'Pigmy' flints found in the British Isles. Were they made by tiny people, as toys for children, or for some other and more obscure reason? Whatever the answer, the standard of workmanship is astonishing for the scale of the objects themselves

Paluxy River in Texas, fossil dinosaur tracks have been found alongside what appear to be fully human footprints – though they are footprints 15 inches (38 centimetres) long.

Chipping flint axes and knives is an aspect of 'ancient technology' that might seem more familiar and comfortable to academic students than the more exotic speculations about ancient bullet wounds and surgery, prehistoric iron nails and golden threads that have been discussed so far. Yet there are some disconcerting artefacts among the countless thousands of flint tools that have been collected since archaeology has been seriously pursued. In Britain, southern Africa, Australia and India, thousands of so-called 'pigmy flints' have been discovered: minute chipped flints in the form of pointed borers, scrapers, and knives. A British antiquarian, Reginald A. Gatty, wrote in 1896 of his own collection:

> . . . when you get down to very minute sizes, to little well-formed flints less than a quarter of an inch [6 millimetres], you need a magnifying glass to discover the workmanship. What hands, what eyes, these prehistoric flint-makers must have had to frame such delicate tools! . . . when seen together, row after row, you realise that these flints were fabricated with a design and purpose, and whoever the people were who made them, dwarves or fairies, they certainly were handicraftsmen of no mean order.

The name 'pigmy flint' is evocative. But, though they were very short by modern standards, there is no evidence that the ancient inhabitants of Britain were literally of pigmy stature – or that they were dwarves or fairies, either. On the other hand, what possible use could these minute implements have for someone of size comparable to our own? And there is no shortage of legends of fairies; and there is that footprint from the Paluxy River suggesting that there might once have been giants on the Earth . . .

This figure is from the Peruvian Mochica culture, which flourished during the first few centuries of the Christian era – at the same time as the civilisation that drew the lines on the Nazca plain. The model apparently shows a child being given an enema

Secrets of the master builders

How was it possible for primitive societies to build stupendous monuments such as Stonehenge, the statues of Easter Island, the stone cities of the Andes and the pyramids of Egypt?

THE TECHNICAL FEAT that made possible the building of Stonehenge and the other megalithic structures of northern Europe is quite stupendous. And the claims that have been made by modern writers about the people who built them are no less impressive. The circle of massive arches at Stonehenge dates from around 1750 BC. It is made up of 'sarsen stones' weighing about 50 tonnes each, brought from the Marlborough Downs about 20 miles (30 kilometres) to the north. One estimate puts the work of construction at $5\frac{1}{4}$ years for 1500 men.

The site was already ancient when the sarsens were erected. The bluestones, forming a double circle, had been brought to Salisbury Plain from the Prescelly Mountains of South Wales some five centuries previously. Weighing about 4 tonnes each, some 82 of them had been brought on boats or rafts by sea and river, with two overland journeys of a few miles to their present location. The feasibility of the journey was established in 1954 when 4-tonne blocks of concrete were transported in exactly the same way over that route. The blocks required 64 men to haul them on sleds and rollers – the largest, the so-called Altar Stone, required 110. Methods by which the standing stones could be set upright, and the lintels lifted onto them, using only Bronze Age tools, have also been worked out.

Stonehenge abounds in mysteries, but these do not lie in the engineering that was employed in it. What was the importance of the site, which was a religious centre from 2500 BC onwards – an importance so great that stones had to be transported hundreds of miles to that particular place? Which of the numerous astronomical alignments that have been found in the structure are genuine and which are merely the result of chance? And what was the significance of the genuine

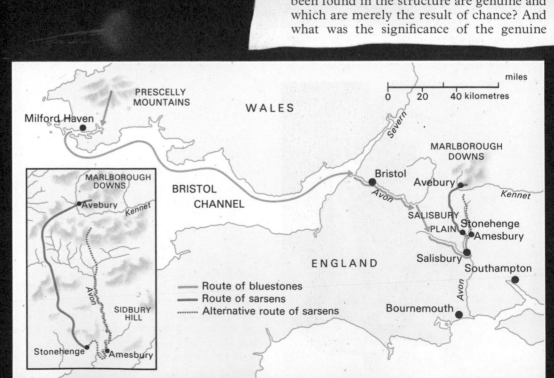

PRESCELLY MOUNTAINS

Milford Haven

WALES

miles
0   20   40 kilometres

MARLBOROUGH DOWNS

Bristol

Avebury

Kennet

BRISTOL CHANNEL

Avon

SALISBURY PLAIN

Stonehenge

Amesbury

Salisbury

ENGLAND

Southampton

Avon

Bournemouth

MARLBOROUGH DOWNS

Avebury

Kennet

Avon

SIDBURY HILL

Stonehenge   Amesbury

—— Route of bluestones
—— Route of sarsens
······ Alternative route of sarsens

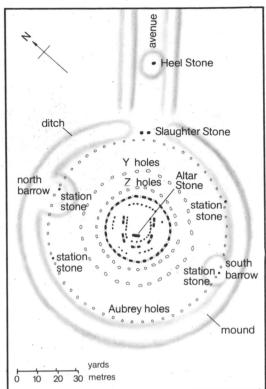

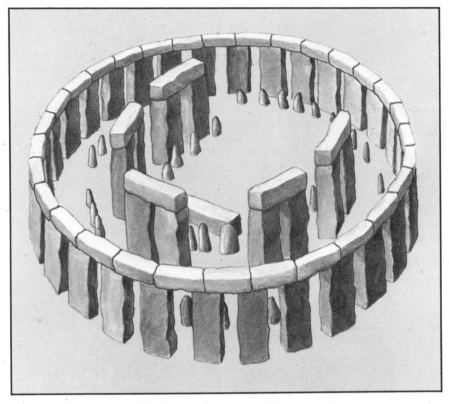

Above: how Stonehenge looked around 1400 BC

Left: routes by which it is thought the megaliths were brought to Stonehenge

Below: the raising of the megaliths. First the uprights were levered into place; then the lintels were placed on platforms and gradually edged higher, then finally eased into position

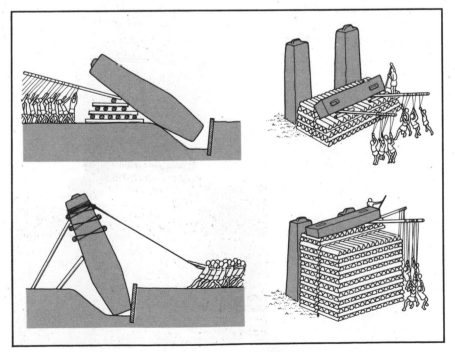

ones, to which the ancient builders devoted so much attention and skilful labour? Was the positioning of the stones also determined by underground streams and other 'water lines', allegedly detected by several dowsers including the late Guy Underwood? Mysteries aplenty, but nothing to justify Rene Noorbergen's question – never directly answered by him – 'Is it possible that the . . . science of the antediluvians [as it survived at the time of Stonehenge] included a method of overcoming the law of gravity?'

There are dangers in attempting to reconstruct the methods used by builders in the past, however – dangers of being too enthusiastic about a favoured technique without rigorous experimental verification, or of jumping to conclusions from unrepresentative small-scale experiments. The Norwegian explorer Thor Heyerdahl may have been guilty of this when he attempted to repeat the achievement of the Easter Island statue-builders.

Easter Island is a remote speck in the Pacific Ocean, the most easterly of the Polynesian islands. The island is covered with the famous, unique statues, with their giant heads and legless bodies. At least 1000 of them are now known, some still lying in the quarries from which they were never removed, others lying damaged in various places, but most gazing out over the rocky, infertile island. Standing between 12 and 15 feet (4 and 5 metres) high, many of them weigh 20 tonnes. How were these monsters moved to their final resting places?

Heyerdahl attempted to answer this question in 1956. He organised a dozen inhabitants of the island to move a head some distance and erect it. It took them 18 days, but they succeeded in the end.

Gods that walked?
This achievement can justly be criticised as a contribution to solving the Easter Island enigma. The head that was moved was one of the smaller ones; it weighed less than 15 tonnes. It was moved only about 100 yards (90 metres) across smooth, sandy ground, with the help of modern ropes. This has little relevance to the 4-mile (6.5-kilometre) journey made by the largest of the island's statues, a giant of 80 tonnes. The statues also

raft the Kon-Tiki because he believed the same people sailed westward to establish the statue-building society of Easter Island. Thus they link the supposed near-magical skills of the Easter Islanders with the super-technology that seems to be spoken of by the ruins of Tiahuanaco.

Heyerdahl believes the early colonists used balsa rafts, and does not credit the story of ancient spacemen. Erich von Däniken, on the other hand, claims that four-fingered beings seen in rock pictures at Tiahuanaco are representations of four-fingered ancestors who arrived from space. To end such speculations, it may need some archaeologist to demonstrate the feasibility of conventional explanations by actually organising the

were undamaged when finally erected, whereas Heyerdahl's team damaged the head of the statue they moved while setting it up.

But neither armchair theorisings nor the small-scale trials of Heyerdahl and others can quite lay to rest the doubts inspired by the awesome landscape of Easter Island – the thought that those ancient gods (if that is what they were) 'walked' to their final homes by means not understood by us.

Ingenuity must be stretched even further to devise means by which the cities and fortresses of the high Andes could have been built. Tiahuanaco lies 13,000 feet (4000 metres) above sea level, an altitude that taxes the lungs of visitors who are not mountain-dwellers. The city, lying just within the Bolivian border, overlooks Lake Titicaca. Nobody knows exactly when it was built – perhaps between AD 200 and 600, perhaps somewhat later. Its temples are massive and intimidating. The blocks from which they are carved are massive – some are 100 tonnes in weight. The quarries from which they come have been located – and they are between 60 and 200 miles (100 and 300 kilometres) distant.

Slaves and freemen?

There are no pictures showing the construction process. Some of the stone, at least, was brought across the lake, in the season when its waters were at their highest. But others must have come by land; perhaps ramps, lubricated with wet clay, would have been constructed to get the stones over slopes. The assumption of conventional thought is that this, or something like it, *must* have been the method used. We know so little of the society that built Tiahuanaco that it is possible to assume that huge numbers of slaves or freemen would have been available to drag the blocks.

But unconventional theorists cannot be blamed for dismissing these conjectures and pointing to the legends of the Incas, as told to the Spanish in the 16th century. They stated that Tiahuanaco was built by a white-skinned, bearded race, led by the god Tikki Viracocha. Thor Heyerdahl named his balsa

Were the Easter Island statues gods that 'walked' to their present sites? Thor Heyerdahl attempted to prove that this was not the case when, in 1956, he persuaded a dozen islanders to move one of the statues from the quarry where it had lain since it was carved, and erect it. In the end they succeeded, although they damaged the statue in the process. It has been pointed out, however, that this experiment is far from proving that this was, indeed, the way that the statues were raised: Heyerdahl's islanders used modern ropes and, perhaps a still more damning fact, the statue they moved was one of the smallest – a mere 15 tonnes as compared to the 80-odd tonnes of the largest statue. To move this would be a formidable task, even using modern ropes

The existence of ancient engineering achievements, vast in scale, has sometimes remained unsuspected by archaeologists intent on other matters. The extensive canal system of the Mayas is a case in point. Until the late 1970s only a few such canals were known. Then a new type of radar, developed to survey the surface of the planet Venus, was used to search for Mayan sites. Carried on flights over central America, the radar revealed networks of lines clustering along rivers and around swamps. Study on the ground confirmed that the features were remains of a canal

A hidden network

system for drainage and irrigation.

The canals were built in pairs, the excavated earth being thrown into the space enclosed by each pair to form a raised island, on which crops were grown. The system ensured that the crops received neither too much nor too little water. The canals permitted an efficient, high-yielding agriculture that supported a population of over 2 million. The Mayan civilisation flourished for over a thousand years until it suddenly collapsed about AD 900 – perhaps because flood or drought caused the failure of the canal system.

transportation of a 100-tonne block over 100 miles (160 kilometres) of rough ground, through forests and across river gorges.

As the only one of the Seven Wonders of the ancient world still standing, the Great Pyramid at Gîza, a few miles south-west of Cairo, has been the object of speculation for centuries. It was built in the 26th century BC for the Pharaoh Cheops (or Khufu). It rises 450 feet (137 metres) above the levelled bedrock, and its base covers an area of 13 acres (5.2 hectares). It is estimated that the pyramid is made up of 2,500,000 sandstone blocks, weighing about 6.5 million tonnes. When it was first built, the royal tomb sparkled white in the brilliant Egyptian sunlight, for it was faced with smooth limestone slabs, long since stolen.

How was the structure raised? Such writers as Rene Noorbergen and Erich von Däniken claim that 2½ million blocks with an average weight of 2.5 tonnes could not have been transported and manipulated into place by 100,000 men (the figure reported by the Greek historian Herodotus) in the 22 years of Cheops's reign. In a flurry of unsupported statistics, Noorbergen concludes that we are speaking of a project that required almost one million people . . .

The Great Pyramid at Gîza. Built 46 centuries ago as a tomb for the Pharaoh Cheops, it is a stupendous feat of science and organisation – but does it provide evidence, as writer Rene Noorbergen supposes, that the pyramids date from before the Flood and were built using some lost super-technology?

one-third to one half the estimated population of all of Egypt around 2700 BC.

Does this sound even remotely reasonable? Not really. There has to be something unreasonable about a calculation that leads to the conclusion that eight man-years are required to cut, transport and position *each* block in the pyramid – even though this figure includes the workers' families and the soldiers allegedly required to police the workers.

Noorbergen also makes much of the quantities of timber required for the barges that floated the blocks down the Nile from as far away as Aswan, a distance of 600 miles (960 kilometres), and for the sledges or rollers with which they were dragged into position. He reports that 'mathematicians tell us 26 million trees would have been required to fashion the necessary number of sledges and rafts.'

Ten trees for each block? That would indeed be extravagant – but perhaps it is the unnamed 'mathematicians' who are at fault. (Most of the sandstone core of the Great Pyramid was in fact cut from local rock, so that it did not need to be brought long distances.)

While this is certainly interesting, Noorbergen's arguments are but a thin thread on which to hang, as he does, the claim that the pyramids date from before the Flood and were constructed with a lost super-technology. In fact, the development of Egyptian building techniques by trial and error can be traced through the centuries.

The achievements of ancient builders can provoke the thought that they could command enormous forces of which we know nothing. But on the whole it is more likely that they could call on only those forces that are the common property of the human race – will-power, intelligence and skills born of experience. Against this background, however, certain anomalies stand out – anomalies such as electrical batteries 1500 years old, and metal artefacts in 'impossible' locations in ancient rocks – that remain to intrigue the speculative mind.

Lyonesse – the magical land west of Land's End to which, so the legend goes, the mortally wounded King Arthur was taken after his last battle – has long been thought to exist only in the imagination. But, argues PAUL BEGG, it may indeed have been a real place

THE LEGEND OF THE LOST LAND of Lyonesse is as confused as it is beautiful. In ancient days, so the local legend goes, Lyonesse was a country that extended westwards from Land's End in Cornwall, connecting the Scilly Isles – which were then linked, forming one big island – with the mainland of England. One hundred and forty parish churches existed there, in good and prosperous farmland, and there were a number of fair-sized towns. It is said that fishermen have pulled up stones from the buildings of Lyonesse in their nets, and that to this day the bells of long-submerged churches can be

projected work on Camelot in 1842, wrote this lyrical account of Lyonesse, adding to the confusion by siting Camelot there:

On the latest limits of the West in the land of Lyonesse, where, save the rocky isles of Scilly all is now wild sea, rose the sacred Mount of Camelot. . . . The Mount was the most beautiful in the world, sometimes green and fresh in the beam of morning, sometimes all one splendour, folded in the golden mists of the West. But all underneath it was hollow, and the mountains trembled when the seas rushed bellowing through the porphyry caves; and there ran a prophecy that the mountain on some wild morning would topple into the abyss and be no more.

More recent reports suggest that memories of the real Lyonesse are still somehow stored at its site.

In the 1930s Stanley Baron, a journalist working for the London *News Chronicle*, is said to have heard bells when staying at

The lost isle of Lyonesse

heard on still nights.

Some poetic stories are set in Lyonesse. It was allegedly the home of Tristram, lover of Isolde, and when it was submerged the only person to escape was a man called Trevilian, who jumped on a white horse and rode to safety. The crest of the Trevelyan family still shows a white horse galloping just ahead of the onrushing waves. Tennyson, outlining a

Sennen Cove, immediately to the north of Land's End. At 1 a.m. one day he was awakened by a rhythmic clanging that persisted for two hours. Later the bells woke him again, and the muffled peal continued until dawn. When he asked his hosts the origin of the sound, they told him that it was the bells of Lyonesse.

Even more startling was a vision seen and

Above: an aerial view of the rocky promontory of Land's End, the extreme western tip of Cornwall. Local legend relates that a stretch of land once joined Land's End to the Scilly Isles (below) – the magical Lyonesse

Right: Edith Olivier who, standing on the cliffs at Land's End, allegedly saw some of the domes and spires of Lyonesse

reported by Edith Olivier, a sometime mayor of Wilton, near Salisbury. Standing on the cliffs of Land's End, she saw a jumble of spires, towers, domes and battlements in the sea!

Edith Olivier's vision may be dismissed as the product of an over-active imagination, but standing on the cliffs of Land's End it is certainly possible to find oneself entranced by the legend of Lyonesse. In the 19th century many artists were attracted by the 'mystical' quality of the light of the Atlantic seaboard, and standing on the cliffs, with the distant Isles of Scilly bathed in the rays of a dying Sun, one can easily believe that the lost land once existed and imagine the catastrophe that swept it beneath the sea. 'On a stormy day at Land's End,' wrote the Poet Laureate, Sir John Betjeman, 'when the two seas collide – the Atlantic Ocean and the English Channel – the waves seem mountains high and one wonders that even the granite can stand up against their force and that the rugged peninsulas survive.'

At one time the Scilly Isles were joined to the mainland by dry land, but that was well before Man trod the Earth. This seems disappointing, for how could a legend recall an event that occurred before Man existed? Yet, like so many persistent legends, the story of the disappearance of Lyonesse may recall a genuine catastrophe. Geologists believe that once upon a time, perhaps within recorded history, there was one large Scilly Isle, perhaps surrounded by a few rocky islets, and it is possible that the Lyonesse story recalls a time when the sea made a dramatic inroad and swamped the land, leaving only the mountain tops – the present

islands – above the level of the water.

The Scilly Isles are a group of about 140 small granitic islands and islets lying 28 miles (45 kilometres) west-south-west of Land's End. Chief among them are St Mary's, Tresco, St Martin's, St Agnes and Bryher. 'A small sweet world of wave-encompassed wonder,' the poet Swinburne called them. The many sailors who have been wrecked or almost wrecked in those treacherous waters have, no doubt, described the Scillies in equally colourful, but perhaps less poetic, language.

The richness of archaeological remains testifies to the importance of the islands in prehistoric times. The islands have over 50 megaliths, a figure disproportionate to the area – Cornwall, for example, has only 17. It has been suggested that the Scillies may have been islands sacred to the dead and that the megaliths may mark the burial places of kings and princes of the mainland. It was once widely believed that spirits of the dead could not cross water, so that to bury a dead

any clues it might hold. This concerns a mysterious island or islands from which the Phoenician traders obtained supplies of tin, and which the Greeks called the Cassiterides.

The Phoenicians were extremely secretive about their supply of tin and left no indication as to the location of the Cassiterides. Some clues are provided by the travels of a man called Pytheas of Massalia – Marseilles – who, two or three hundred years before Christ, followed the Phoenicians' trade routes. Nothing is known for certain about him, and his voyage cannot be more precisely dated than some time between 310 and 238 BC, but it is now generally accepted that he journeyed around Britain. Indeed, on the grounds that the Phoenicians had no real idea of the extent of the British Isles, Pytheas is sometimes credited with the discovery of Britain. His own account of the voyage no longer exists, but was used as source material by many writers, among them Diodorus Siculus and Strabo.

chief on the islands would have been a sure way of preventing his return to his kingdom, where he could cause problems for his successor. It may have been the dim local tradition of the Scillies being 'sacred isles' that gave rise to the legend that King Arthur was rowed out to the west to Lyonesse after the fatal battle of Camlann. Another explanation is that if the Scillies *were* once a single island, their population might have been much larger – larger perhaps even than Cornwall's – and the large number of megaliths would no longer seem surprising, particularly if, being out of touch with the mainland, the early Scillonians continued to use megaliths long after the practice had ceased elsewhere.

Perishable remains

It is pointed out by some experts that the inundation of the Scillies would have been well-documented had it happened in historic times and that, since no such documents have been found, there can have been no inundation. However, this is not necessarily true: the Romans and Anglo-Saxons never occupied Cornwall effectively so, even if they had heard the legend of Lyonesse, they might not have attached any significance to it. Also, the common writing material of the period was papyrus, which perishes all too easily in the damp British climate. By the early medieval period all we might expect to find are records of a garbled oral tradition – and that is exactly what we have.

For reliable information we must turn to archaeology and geology, but there is one body of written material worth examining for

Megalithic monuments on the Scilly Isles: a burial chamber on Little Arthur (top) and a row of standing stones on St Mary's (above). The Scilly Isles have an exceptionally large number of such monuments – which has led some experts to suggest that the population of the Scillies must once have been far larger than it is now

Strabo (63 BC-AD 21), a Greek historian and geographer, wrote that the Cassiterides were

opposite the west parts of Britain, situate as it were in the same climate with Britain, are ten in number and lie near each other, in the ocean toward the north from the haven of Artabri. One of them is a desert, but the others are inhabited by men in black cloaks, clad in tunics reaching to the feet, girt about the breast, and walking with staves.

Strabo, then is quite clear that the Cassiterides were not a single island, but numbered 10 and were situated opposite the west of Britain. The position certainly fits the Scilly Isles in everything but number.

Diodorus Siculus, a Sicilian-Greek historian writing about the time of the Emperor Augustus (27 BC-AD 14), described Britain as triangular in shape and assigned to the vertices of the triangle the names Kantion, Orka and Belerion. Kantion is Kent, and Orka is clearly the northern tip of Scotland opposite the Orkney Islands, so by elimination Belerion must be the ancient native name for Land's End. Diodorus writes:

The natives of Britain near the headland of Belerion are unusually friendly and through intercourse with foreign traders have become very mannerly. They have a clever process for extracting tin from its bed . . . . After they have smelted and refined the tin they hammer it into the shape of knuckle-bones and transport it to an adjoining island named Iktis. Having waited for the ebb tides to lay bare the intervening channel, they bring entire loads of tin across on wagons. Now there is a peculiar phenomenon connected with the neighbouring islands. I mean those that lie between Europe and Britain, for at the flood tide the intervening passage is overflowed, and they seem like islands, but a large space is left dry at the ebb and they seem to be like peninsulas.

Dangerous anchorage

Diodorus's words have been interpreted to mean that the natives of Cornwall (Belerion) mined tin – that Cornwall is therefore probably the Cassiterides – and transported it by wagon at ebb tide to the island of Iktis. Iktis has been identified as the picturesque St Michael's Mount, which rises precipitously to a height of 230 feet (70 metres) from Mount's Bay and at low water can be reached by a causeway from Marazion. However, without the modern quay, St Michael's Mount would have been an extremely dangerous anchorage affording little shelter and is therefore an odd place for the traders to choose to draw up their ships.

Another objection to the identification of the Cassiterides as mainland Cornwall is that

Above: the Greek historian and geographer Strabo (63 BC–AD 21), who gives an account of the Cassiterides, a group of 10 islands 'opposite the west parts of Britain'. This description fits the Scilly Isles – in everything but number

Below: St Michael's Mount, near Marazion in Cornwall. A first-century AD account refers to an island named Iktis, which some historians have identified as St Michael's Mount. Others, however, have suggested that Iktis is in fact the Scilly Isles, then a single island – perhaps the original Lyonesse

this hardly fits Strabo's description of 10 islands. It seems far more reasonable to suppose that Diodorus is referring to the Scillies, but if so, he is saying that they could be reached from the mainland over dry land at ebb tide. This most certainly isn't possible today, and geologists are adamant that it hasn't been possible since prehistoric times.

'The natives of Britain *near* the headlands of Belerion . . . .' Could Diodorus's opening statement refer to the natives of Britain who lived on Scilly *near the headlands of Belerion*? It fits Strabo's location of the Cassiterides as 'opposite the west parts of Britain' and being 'ten in number' (more will be said about the number) and, if the interpretation is correct, early descriptions of the Cassiterides indicate that there was once a large Isle of Scilly surrounded by nine lesser isles, one of which was Iktis, and that all were joined together at ebb tide.

One of the objections to the identification of the Cassiterides with the Scilly Isles is the opinion of geologists that the islands were never very rich in tin. However, early accounts may suggest that tin existed near the surface, the early mining pits therefore being shallow and soon lost once they were no longer in use. There are references to tin being mined, or of its availability for mining, in 1563. In 1750 an army officer named Robert Heath reported that in 1744 a 'miner discovered a rich vein of ore, which promised encouragement for working.'

Finally, it should be noted that there are two very early descriptions of the Scilly Isles, one in the *Polyhistor* written by Solinus about AD 240, the other by Sulpicius Severus, writing about AD 400. Significantly, they both refer to Scilly in the singular – *Siluram insulam*!

The city under the sea

The chronicles of western Cornwall refer again and again to a land called Lyonesse that stretched westwards from Land's End. What was its exact location, and how did it disappear?

THE EARLIEST MENTION of Lyonesse is to be found in the *Itinery* of William Worcestre written in 1480. Between 1478 and 1480 William made several journeys through England, making numerous notes of what he saw, read and was told. His *Itinery* is therefore a valuable source of jottings on people, places, buildings, ecology and natural history – and on something that evidently particulary fascinated William, history and historical traditions. Of the vague Cornish traditions of a vision of St Michael the Archangel at St Michael's Mount, which Worcestre dates as having happened in the year 710, he writes:

> The apparition of St Michael at the Mountain tomb, formerly called the Hoar Rock in the Wood; and there were both woods and meadows and plough-land between the said mount and the Scilly Isles and 140 parish churches were drowned between that mount and Scilly. . . . The site of St Michael's Mount is . . . surrounded by the ocean; and the monks of the same place [asked] the Bishop of Avranches, named Aubert, to build a temple of St Michael; the aforesaid place was formerly clad in densest forest, six miles [10

An aerial view of the Scilly Isles, showing clearly the shallowness of the sea between them. Could it be that the Scillies were once one large island – subsequently immortalised in legend as Lyonesse?

kilometres] from the sea, and offered a most suitable retreat for wild beasts, where we find there were formerly monks serving God.

Aubert, Bishop of Avranches, in north-west France, is unknown beyond the legend that between 706 and 708 he three times fell asleep on the Rocher de la Tombe, a rocky island off the coast close to Avranches, and each time saw a vision of St Michael, who told him to build a church in that place. Bishop Aubert – who was later canonised – did so, and the church of Mont Saint Michel was the result. St Aubert was buried there about 725.

It has been argued that William Worcestre must have based his account on copies of manuscripts he saw in the abbey of Mont Saint Michel, confusing the legend of Lyonesse with stories current in Normandy about great inundations along the Atlantic coast of France; the best-known of these tells of the splendid city of Ys that was said once to have existed on the shores of what is now the Bay of Douarnenez. However, there are some important pieces of evidence to suggest that Worcestre's account may be accurate. A petrified forest has been found around the base of St Michael's Mount, so it seems feasible that the mount should once have been known, as Worcestre claims, as the Hoar Rock in the Wood. A site where axes were made, dating from around 1500 BC, has been discovered in Mount's Bay, which means that the area around the mount must once have been above water, and Worcestre's report that the mount and the Scilly Isles were once joined by a tract of land may be correct.

Another important mention of Lyonesse comes in the *Description of Cornwall* published by the famous map-maker John Norden in 1584; and 18 years later, in his *Survey of Cornwall*, Richard Carew provides details that have since become a standard part of the legend:

the encroaching sea hath ravined from it the whole country of Lyonesse, together with divers other parcels of no little circuit, and that such a Lyonesse there was these proofs are yet remaining. The space between Land's End and the Isles of Scilly, being about thirty miles [50 kilometres], to this day retaineth the name, in Cornish *Lethowsow*, and carrieth continually an equal depth of 40–60 fathom [60 to 100 metres] (a thing not unproper in the sea's proper dominion) save that about midway there lieth a rock which at low tide discovereth his head. They term it the Gulf, suiting thereby the other name of Scilla. Fishermen also casting their hooks thereabouts have drawn up pieces of doors and windows. Moreover, the ancient name of St Michael's Mount was Cara-clowse in Cowse, in

Below: the Bay of Douarnenez, close to Mont Saint Michel (bottom) in north-west France, possibly the site of the legendary city of Ys which, so the story goes, was swept away by floods. A 15th-century account by William Worcestre tells of a land that once stretched between St Michael's Mount in Cornwall and the Scilly Isles. Is this a reference to Lyonesse – or is Worcestre simply muddling St Michael's Mount with Mont Saint Michel and the stories of the disappearance of Ys with similar stories of Lyonesse?

extremity of Cornwall, there is the base of an old stone column, belonging to a building, which was taken up by some fishermen about the place of the Seven Stones, about 18 inches [50 centimetres] height and three feet [1 metre] diameter at the circular base. Besides which, other pieces of building and glass windoes have been taken up at different times in the same place, with divers kind of utensils.

Some interesting ruins are mentioned by the Reverend William Borlase in an article with the title 'Of the great alterations which the islands of Scilly have undergone since the time of the ancients', published in the *Philosophical Transactions* of 1754:

The flats which stretch from one island to another, are plain evidences of a former union subsisting between many now distinct islands. The flats between Trescaw, Brehar and Samson are quite dry at spring tide, and men easily pass dry-shod from one island to another, over sand banks (where, on the shifting of the sands, walls and ruins are frequently discovered) on which at full sea there are 10 and 12 feet [3 or 4 metres] of water.

Herbs and incantations

A quarter of a century after Borlase, in 1780, an old Cornishwoman is said to have poured a selection of herbs into the sea at Land's End and spoken an incantation that, she hoped, would result in Lyonesse rising from the waves. Nothing happened, of course – but in one sense, just over a century later, perhaps Lyonesse did begin to rise, from the realms of legend into the world of fact. In an article, 'Lyonesse', in the journal *Antiquity* in 1927, archaeologist O.G.S. Crawford wrote how, while walking at the spring tide across the

English, the Hoar Rock in the Wood, which now is at every flood encompassed by the sea, and yet at some low ebbs, roots of mighty trees are described in the sands about it.

If the fishermen *did* bring up 'pieces of doors and windows' from around the region of the Seven Stones reef, such flotsam is likely to have come from one of the many wrecks in the area. However, the assertion is repeated 150 years later, in 1750, with a very interesting addition by Robert Heath in his *A natural and historical account of the islands of Scilly*:

At Sennen Church-Town, near the

sandflats between Samson and Tresco, he and a companion found a line of stones – probably the very stones mentioned by Borlase:

> We found that the line of stones was undoubtedly the remains of a wall of human construction. It consisted of boulders and stones about the size of a milestone, some of them still standing upright. All round on either side of the wall were scattered the smaller stones which once filled the spaces between the larger uprights. Elsewhere the sands were almost bare. The fact that some of these stones still remained standing proved conclusively that the thing was artificial.

The line of boulders discovered by Crawford was the remnant of a stone dyke, and it must have been built at a time when the region now under water was dry land. It provides important evidence to support the view that the sea level has risen since the emergence of agricultural Man – and perhaps within recorded history.

In fact, hydrographers have now confirmed that the Isles of Scilly were once a single, large island. At the 65-foot (18-metre) line the present islands are revealed as the hills of an island some 7 miles (11 kilometres) long and 6 miles (10 kilometres) wide with a long, narrow peninsula pushing out for about

The story of Tristram

The story of Tristram of Lohnis – Lyonesse – and Isolde, or Yseult, is among the most tragic and moving episodes of the Arthurian cycle. Tristram, the orphaned son of the king of Lohnis, is adopted as a baby by King Mark. Years later, he is sent to Ireland to collect Mark's bride, Isolde 'the fair', daughter of the Irish king Gurman. On the journey back to Cornwall there is an accident with a love potion intended for the use of Mark and Isolde on their wedding night. Against their inclinations, and despite their obligations to Mark, Tristram and Isolde fall irresistibly in love and are eventually destroyed by the conflict of their passion for each other and their loyalties and obligations to Mark.

It is a tragic and beautiful story, but one question remains: does Tristram really have any connection with Lyonesse? Some authorities believe that the Tristram-Isolde story was based on a factual account of the life of Drust – an early form of the name Tristram – son of a Pictish king named Tallorc who ruled about 780. It is argued that Lohnis

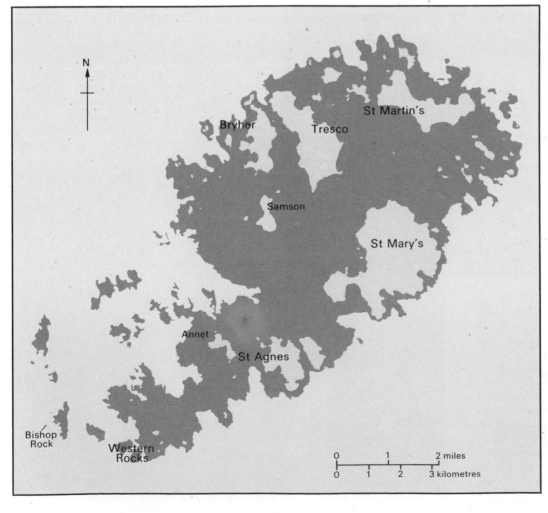

Left: a map of the Scilly Isles. The green area represents the islands as they appear at high tide; the grey area is that which would be uncovered if the sea level were to sink by 65 feet (20 metres). Some experts have argued that the legend of Lyonesse originates from a time when the sea level was this low, and the Scilly Islands formed a single land mass

was not Lyonesse, but Drust's home – Lothian in Scotland.

However, a mile (1.6 kilometres) north-west of Fowey in Cornwall there stands a monolith bearing the inscription *Drustanus hic iacit filius Cunomori* ('Here lies Tristram, son of Cynvawr'). It is known that a sixth-century king of Cornwall was named Cynvawr, and it is reasonable to assume that the Tristram important enough to be commemorated by a monolith was his son. A ninth-century manuscript written by a monk of Llandevennec named Wrmonoc records that a sixth-century king of Brittany named Mark was also called Cynvawr. It is perfectly possible that this king of Brittany's rule extended to Cornwall and that he and the Cornish king are one and the same. Thus we have a real Tristram, who was probably the son – perhaps adopted – of a King Mark, and was a contemporary of Arthur.

Lyonesse, if it existed, was almost certainly submerged by Tristram's time, so it is unlikely to have been his home, but it remains possible that his family originally came from whatever part may have remained above water – that is, the Scilly Isles.

This seaweed-covered wall, uncovered at low tide on the sandflats between the islands of Samson and Tresco, suggests that the land on which it stands was once always above water

occurred as late as around AD 370, it could not only have given rise to the legend of Lyonesse, but also have become part of the Tristram story (see box) very early in its development.

Demonstration that the sea level has risen dramatically within historical time does not, of course, necessarily make the story of the sudden submergence of Lyonesse any less of a myth, but it does show that it may have a factual foundation. It is not difficult to imagine the depth of feeling that such a disaster would have engendered. Homes were destroyed, farmland was submerged, lives were no doubt lost. And as the memory was passed from one generation to the next, so the extent of the remembered destruction was magnified.

And perhaps that old Cornishwoman's mixture of herbs is beginning to make Lyonesse rise again in a more tangible way. In his *The geology of the Scilly Isles*, George Barrow writes:

> One point has been established in the clearest manner: the area above water in the Scilly Isles has not diminished in recent times, but has distinctly increased; and this increase is due to the constant washing up of the fine sand from the shallow sea-floor . . . .

If the Scilly Isles were once Lyonesse, then it could be said that Lyonesse is rising!

3 miles (5 kilometres) westwards in the direction of Bishop Rock. This is how the Scilly Isles must have looked about 8000 BC, at the end of the last glacial period. Successive centuries saw the sea level rise. By 500 BC the Western Isles, Annet and Agnes – eight or nine islands altogether – had become separated from the main island. The sea level went on rising and there were a few dramatic inundations. Then, about AD 370, there occurred the final great submergence, which left the Scillies in their present form.

Among the most recently found evidence for this picture of the Scilly Isles are the remains of a settlement discovered on one of the smallest of the Eastern Isles, Nornour. The existence of this settlement was unknown before 1962, but the spring storms of that year revealed a wall, and subsequent excavation uncovered a number of rooms that had been continuously occupied from the late period of the megalith builders until approximately the fourth century AD. The Nornour site shows clear evidence of a gradual submergence, although the sea does not appear to have made any significant inroads from about the second century BC until around AD 370.

This description of the Scillies fits very well with how it may have looked in the time of Pytheas of Massalia and with Strabo's description of the Cassiterides (see page 50). It also fits the description given by Solinus and Sulpicius Severus of the Scillies as a single island. And if the final inundation

One of the best-known heroes of all time is King Arthur, saviour of Britain, 'the once and future king'. PAUL BEGG tells of his legendary exploits and investigates the timeless appeal of the Arthurian romances

THE MERE MENTION of King Arthur and the Round Table is enough to conjure up images of gallantry and romance: towering castles, white chargers, flashing sword blades . . . This is the very stuff of childhood dreams and the inspiration of generations of poets and artists. The names of those champions of chivalry: Arthur, Bedivere, Galahad, Gawain, Lancelot, Perceval, Tristram, Galahad; they are imbued with a singular vibrancy and resonance, which has echoed down the centuries.

It was at a great feast in London that Uther Pendragon, King of England, first set eyes on the beautiful Ygraine (sometimes called Igerna), the wife of his trusted friend and most loyal supporter Gorlois, Duke of Cornwall, and was immediately overcome by the desire to possess her. His intentions were perceived by Gorlois, who shut Ygraine away in the impregnable castle at Tintagel. Beside himself with passion, Uther sought the help of Merlin, the master magician, and was given a potion that made him look exactly like Gorlois. Thus disguised, Uther had no trouble entering Tintagel Castle and Ygraine's bed. That night Arthur was conceived – and that same night Gorlois was killed by Uther's men. Uther and Ygraine promptly married.

Merlin claimed the newborn Arthur and entrusted him to the care of a knight named

Right: Uther Pendragon and the magician Merlin plot the ravishing of Ygraine, wife of Gorlois, Duke of Cornwall, as she looks on with misgiving – an illustration from the medieval *Chronicle of England* by Peter of Langtoft

Below: the ruins of Tintagel Castle in Cornwall. It was here that, according to legend, Arthur was conceived

Ector, who raised Arthur as his own, the younger brother of his son Kay. When Arthur was almost 15, Merlin summoned the nobility of the land to London. Outside the church where everyone gathered one Sunday for Mass there was a stone with an anvil embedded in it, and protruding from the anvil there was a magnificent sword. Engraved on the stone were the words: WHOSOEVER PULLETH OUT THIS SWORD OF THIS STONE AND ANVIL IS RIGHTWISE KING BORN OF ALL ENGLAND.

Many lords and knights tried to draw the sword from the stone, but all failed to do so. Yet when Arthur tried to draw the sword it slid free without effort. He was proclaimed king, much to the fury of many great nobles, among them Loth of Lothian, and there followed many years of bitter fighting before they accepted Arthur as their king.

To make peace Loth sent his beautiful wife Morgause on an embassy to Arthur. Unaware that she was his half sister, one of three daughters born to Ygraine and Gorlois, Arthur made love to her and she conceived a child. Merlin prophesied that the boy born of

The legend of King Arthur

besmirched. The code of chivalry, which had been the backbone of the Round Table, now became its weakness, propelling the participants on a tide of emotion towards a final, terrible catastrophe they were powerless to avert.

In Arthur's absence Mordred, left in England to tend the kingdom, raised an army and seized the crown. Arthur returned to England and his army eventually met Mordred's forces at Camlann. A terrible battle raged and many of the knights died. Arthur eventually delivered a mortal blow to Mordred, but before he died Mordred struck Arthur with his sword.

Dying, Arthur instructed Bedivere to throw Excalibur into the lake from which it had come. Bedivere hurled the great sword out as far as he could and an arm came out of the water, caught the sword and vanished. The mortally wounded king was then taken to the lake's edge, where a barge waited to carry him to the fairy isle of Avalon – widely believed to be Glastonbury – where it was said that he died. But the people refused to accept that King Arthur was dead and a rumour spread that there was written on his tomb: HIC IACET ARTHURUS REX QUONDAM REXQUE FUTURUS (Here lies Arthur, the once and future king).

This is the story of King Arthur as most people know it, their image perhaps having received additional colour via Hollywood. But where did this romanticised image come from?

It is widely believed, but by no means

Arthur's unwitting incest would bring about the destruction of the kingdom. The child was named Mordred.

Meanwhile, in combat, Arthur had broken the sword drawn from the stone. Merlin had taken him to a lake and there he had been given a magic sword called Excalibur by a powerful fay – someone who possessed magical powers – the Lady of the Lake.

Arthur later married Guinevere and received a magnificent round table as a wedding present. Around this table sat the knights of Arthur's court. However, one seat, the 'Siege Perilous', was left vacant, reserved for the one knight who would succeed in the quintessentially spiritual quest for the Grail, the holiest relic in Christendom.

The adventures of the knights are full of supernatural marvels, but the most important theme in the Arthurian legend is the love affair between Lancelot and Guinevere. They became so indiscreet in their passion for each other that Arthur learned of it and was forced, by Mordred and his peers, to recognise it and accuse the couple publicly of adultery and treason. Lancelot, with Guinevere and many of the knights, fled to France, hotly pursued by Arthur's army. The forces met. Lives were lost and honour

Above: Arthur and his knights on a wild-animal hunt in an illustration by Gustave Doré of Lord Tennyson's epic poem *Idylls of the King*. Together with the romantic paintings of Arthurian legends by the Pre-Raphaelite brotherhood, Tennyson helped to create the popular image of the knights of the Round Table

Right: an early 16th-century illuminated manuscript, Flemish in origin, depicting two knights jousting before Arthur and his court. The winner of the ritual battle was considered to have won a moral as well as physical victory. The victor was also considered exceedingly glamorous, especially as it was believed to be a common practice for the knights to wear ladies' 'favours' – coloured scarves – to the joust and a victory could be seen as a symbolic kill for the lady's sake

proven, that there was a real Arthur active in the late fifth century, but it is an early yet unavoidable disappointment to learn that in history there was no Round Table, no magical castle called Camelot and no Lancelot. These are all medieval inventions. The whole paraphernalia of knighthood, armour, courtly love and epic gallantry is derived from conditions and ideals far removed from those the historic Arthur knew.

The story of Arthur was not born as a single cohesive narrative, but began life as a scattered collection of tales that originally probably had nothing to do with any discernible historical figure. These traditional tales were attached to a heroic figure and subsequently gathered into a single story to which writers added further adventures. The story of Arthur as it has come down to us – through Sir Thomas Malory's *Morte d'Arthur*, Lord Tennyson's *Idylls of the King* and T.H. White's *The once and future king* – is a distillation of these many tales, which are collectively known as the Matter of Britain.

Arthur's fame spreads

The legend developed in the years following the Norman conquest of Britain in 1066. In Wales, Cornwall and Brittany, the Celtic fringe of the Anglo-Norman lands, the stories about Arthur had been preserved and were taken up by wandering minstrels. These storytellers spread the stories far and wide, and by the end of the 11th century Arthur was known throughout Europe. His fame is testified to by a stone carving above the northern doorway of Modena Cathedral in Italy, believed to date from before 1120, depicting a scene from an Arthurian story about the abduction of Guinevere and her rescue by Arthur.

About 1136 a Benedictine monk named Geoffrey of Monmouth gathered the pseudo-historical bardic tales, folklore and traditions and combined them with genuine history, and a little imagination, to weave them into a single, cohesive narrative that he called the *Historia regum Britanniae* ('The history of the kings of Britain'), which has perhaps fairly been described as 'one of the most influential books ever written in this

Above: Arthur celebrated in a mosaic, dating from 1166, in Otranto Cathedral, Italy. Its origins are obscure but it seems likely that the Arthurian legends were taken to Italy by the Normans

Below: opening scenes of the 15th-century illuminated manuscript *Lancelot* showing (top left) the birth of Lancelot; (top right) Lancelot being brought up by the Lady of the Lake; (bottom left) Lancelot at a tournament and (bottom right) his vision of the Holy Grail

country.' Geoffrey presented the *Historia* as a genuine history, saying he had done no more than translate 'a certain very ancient book' that had been given to him by his friend Walter, Archdeacon of Oxford. Whether or not such a book ever really existed is open to debate, but the *Historia* was not a simple, straightforward translation of a single book. And neither was it a genuine history, as several contemporary writers recognised. One critic said that it 'was made up, partly by [Geoffrey] and partly by others, either from an inordinate love of lying, or for the sake of pleasing the Britons'.

The *Historia* begins with the founding of Britain by Brutus, the grandson of Aeneas, hero of Virgil's *Aeneid*, and continues through a long line of kings that includes such familiar names as Lear, Cymbeline and Coel (the Old King Cole of the nursery rhyme), down to Arthur, who occupies a fifth of the book.

Although the *Historia* gives the names of many now familiar people, places and things – Merlin, Guinevere, Mordred, Kay, Bedivere, Tintagel, Camlann, Avalon and Arthur's special sword, here named Caliburn – the story is firmly set in the fifth century and there is no Round Table, Lancelot, Galahad or Holy Grail.

The *Historia* was immensely popular and in it the Norman kings, having by now established their grip on conquered Britain, found a hero who was a worthy rival to Charlemagne, the legends about whom bestowed an enviable lustre on the kings of

court at Camelot; and *Perceval* or *Conte du Graal* (1182), left unfinished after 9000 lines – of which more will be said later. He also wrote a poem about Tristram and Yseult (otherwise known as Isolde), but this has been lost. But what is probably de Troyes's chief contribution is the introduction of the important love affair between Lancelot and Guinevere.

About 1200 a Burgundian knight named Robert de Boron (or Borron) produced what has now become the standard legend of Arthur's early life, developing the importance of Merlin's role in the young hero's career. He also wrote the earliest surviving account of the early history of the Holy Grail and incorporated it into the Arthurian cycle.

Meanwhile, other writers – Thomas of England (*c.* 1160), Eilhart von Oberg (*c.* 1170), Beroul (*c.* 1190) and, of course, Chrétien de Troyes – had been developing the non-Arthurian story of Tristram and Isolde: despite their moral inhibitions and strong loyalties to others, Tristram and Isolde fall passionately in love because of a love potion and are gradually torn apart by their conflicting loyalties. In about 1230 a story called *Le roman de Tristan de Leonis* absorbed Tristram into the Arthurian cycle, making him a knight of the Round Table.

France. Arthur had fought against the Saxons, the Normans had defeated them, and this at least gave the Normans a spiritual brotherhood with the native Britons and everything that Arthur stood for. However, it was in France that the stories about Arthur were developed.

About 1154, Robert Wace, a canon of Bayeux, wrote *Roman de Brut*, a reworking of Geoffrey's *Historia* with poetic amplifications, the most important of which was the introduction of the Round Table, here said to have been devised by Arthur so that no knight should have precedence. Wace says that the Bretons told many tales about the Round Table, but the form these stories took is lost in the mists of time. Later writers developed the theme of the Round Table and it became an exalted order of chivalry.

The single most influential author in the development of the Arthurian romances was Chrétien de Troyes. A Frenchman, it is he more than any other who can be held responsible for having determined the nature and significance of the legends in modern literature. Chrétien wrote several long verse romances: *Erec and Enid* (1170), in which Perceval and Lancelot make their first appearance in Arthurian literature; *Cligès* (1176); *Yvain* and *Lancelot* (both 1177), the latter being the first work to locate Arthur's

Previous page top:
W. Hatherall's painting *The battle between King Arthur and Sir Mordred*, hangs in the so-called King Arthur's Hall, Tintagel

Previous page bottom: the 19th-century vision of the death of Arthur, as epitomised by this tapestry design by Edward Burne-Jones

The enduring fascination with the Arthurian legend in the 20th century is reflected in numerous, if widely different, films. They include (right) the highly irreverent *Monty Python and the Holy Grail* (1975), and (below) the grimly realistic *Excalibur* (1981) starring Nigel Terry as Arthur. Others include Walt Disney's cartoon *The sword in the stone* (1963) and many undistinguished Hollywood movies

Between 1215 and 1230 an influential attempt was made to draw the great many Arthurian stories into a coherent whole in a series of French romances by different authors that are today known as the Vulgate cycle because they are widely regarded as the 'bible' of Arthurian literature. It is here that Galahad makes his first appearance, taking his place in the Siege Perilous.

About 1469 the finest flowering of the Arthurian legend was created under the pen of Sir Thomas Malory, a rogue whose career of violent crime had eventually landed him in Newgate gaol. It was here that he wrote *La morte d'Arthur* – the title was not Malory's, but was bestowed upon the book by William Caxton, who edited and printed it in 1485, 14 years after Malory's death.

The story of Arthur has attracted many writers and artists since Malory, including Edmund Spenser, Alfred Lord Tennyson, the Pre-Raphaelites, John Masefield, T.H. White, and more recently Mary Stewart. The cinema was a little late in taking up the theme and the Arthurian film cycle effectively began with a 15-episode serial produced in 1949, *The adventures of Sir Galahad*. But the Arthurian film really got under way in 1954 with the classic *Prince Valiant*, based on a comic strip created by

Hal Foster. More recently there have been Walt Disney's *The sword in the stone* and the musical *Camelot*, the black comedy *Monty Python and the Holy Grail*, and the attempt to recapture the epic grandeur of the story, *Excalibur*.

Many people have offered theories to explain the deep and timeless appeal of the Arthurian legends. One suggestion worth comment is that underlying the stories runs the theme of supernatural forces controlling destiny. Such a theme most certainly exists, but it is not very inspiring. Uther, a good king, becomes the puppet of destiny when he seduces Ygraine and betrays and brings about the death of Gorlois. Galahad is likewise destined to achieve the quest for the Grail; Lancelot and Perceval are doomed to fail. And Mordred is destined to destroy Arthur and the Round Table. There is a strange, archetypal symbolism here, but watching a great king tumble headlong towards disaster can hardly account for the stories' lasting appeal.

Perhaps the story is a metaphor, the struggles of Arthur and his knights representing the struggles of life in general. Or maybe the answer is simply that whatever the generation, whatever the society, loyalty and honour are highly regarded values, epitomised by the knights of the Round Table. And, of course, there is a nagging desire to believe that somewhere, in some time or place, the whole story was true.

The quest for the Holy Grail

The central, unifying theme of the Arthurian legends is the search for the 'great and precious' vessel – the Holy Grail. But did some deeper meaning lie beneath this mystical quest?

THE HOLY GRAIL is a confused and confusing concept, profound, unorthodox, and apparently not even understood by the Arthurian romancers, none of whom says precisely what it means. The Grail itself is sometimes depicted as a stone, in one bizarre story it is a platter on which rests a human head swimming in blood, elsewhere it is a repository for holy relics, but most often it is the cup or chalice used by Jesus at the Last Supper and in which his blood was caught as he hung upon the cross. Together with the spear with which the centurion pierced Christ's side, the Grail is supposed to have been brought to England by Joseph of Arimathea, the wealthy Jew to whose tomb Jesus was taken from the cross. In the Arthurian romances custody of the Grail was invested in a line of Grail keepers, descendants of Joseph, who preserve it in a mysterious castle.

There is a large literature on the Grail and on its significance in the Arthurian cycle and in Celtic myth. One view is that the story is based on an actual visit to England by either Joseph or his disciples, another that it comes from the same reservoir of Celtic myth as the Arthur story, and a third view is that the Grail stories conceal a secret occult lore or lost knowledge passed down through the initiates of a secret society founded in distant antiquity. This latter idea was itself inspired by G.R.S. Mead's Quest Society, an offshoot of the Theosophist movement founded in the late 19th century by the colourful and formidable Madame Blavatsky.

Of these disparate theories, the first is the most appealing but, alas, one for which there is little, if any, supporting evidence. The third has received short shrift from everyone except those occultists whose beliefs are not hindered by such awkward necessities as evidence, in this case evidence of a secret cult and evidence of an organised 'knowledge' in the Grail cycle. But it is almost certain that the Grail legends were inspired either by a coherent pagan myth or a collection of separate myths about magic vessels of life and regeneration. Different authors took these loosely connected pagan themes and constructed their own particular Grail story.

The earliest surviving story about the Grail is the *Conte du Graal* ('Story of the Grail'), written by Chrétien de Troyes about 1180 and left unfinished after 9000 lines. Chrétien says that he based the story on a

Below: Arthur and his knights set off on their search for the Holy Grail. Their elusive destination and the trials encountered as they continue their quest can be understood on many levels: as a straightforward adventure story in epic style; as a metaphorical description of the problems of life in general; or as the archetypal search for a deeper, spiritual meaning for Man's existence

book given to him by Count Philip of Flanders, which may or may not be true. It should be remembered that these stories were not presented as fiction, but as fact, and great faith was placed in the antiquity of the source as a guarantee of their accuracy. Chrétien and subsequent writers 'invented' sources to explain how they had come by their stories.

The hero is Perceval of Wales and the story includes a Grail castle and Grail keeper, a large platter with mysterious attributes, and other elements contained in many of the Grail stories, such as a question that must be asked in order to heal a wounded king and restore fertility to his land.

The magic cauldron

The character of Perceval is almost certainly derived from the sagas of the Welsh hero Pryderi, almost all that remains of whose stories are to be found in the *Mabinogion*, a collection of early Welsh narratives based on centuries-old oral tales. Several of the stories contain references to a magic cauldron that possesses many of the traditional attributes of the Grail.

The *Mabinogion* preserves much of the primitive, fantastic world of Celtic mythology and also features some early stories about Arthur. In one of these, *The spoils of Annwn*, Arthur and his men sail to the otherworld of Annwn to seize the magic cauldron. Only Arthur and seven of his companions return alive. *The spoils of Annwn* is itself based on an earlier story in the *Mabinogion*: *Branwen, daughter of Llyr*, one of the Pryderi sagas. It is clear that these Celtic heroes are based on much earlier gods

Right: Jesus is taken down from the cross by his followers, wrapped in a single piece of cloth and prepared for burial in the tomb of Joseph of Arimathea, a rich disciple. Joseph was to become the central figure in the legend connecting Glastonbury with the Grail

Below: Joseph, son of Joseph of Arimathea, is consecrated as the first Bishop of Western Christendom. The Grail, however, was shunned by the Church, and its mysteries evolved almost as a separate religion

of pagan mythology. Llyr, for example, is the Celtic equivalent of the Gaelic Ler, a sea god and member of a group of Gaelic gods known as the *Tuatha de Danaan* (Folk of the goddess Danu), who possess a magic cauldron, a spear that is all conquering and a sword that is an infallible weapon, all of which clearly parallel the Arthurian Grail, the spear that pierced Jesus's side, and Excalibur.

About 1200 Robert de Boron wrote a long

poem, *Joseph di Arimathie*, in which he told how the Grail came into the possession of Joseph of Arimathea. Like Chrétien de Troyes, de Boron claimed to have based the story on an earlier source, 'a great book' written by 'great clerks'.

Joseph of Arimathea is a relatively minor character in the New Testament. He was a wealthy Jew and 'a disciple of Jesus, but secretly for fear of the Jews' (John 19:38), in whose tomb Jesus's body was laid when taken from the cross. Joseph's role, however, is expanded in the Apocryphal New Testament, which tells us that the Jews became furious about Joseph's generosity and locked him in a windowless room, intending to kill him later. But before they could do so, the risen Jesus led Joseph to freedom.

Robert de Boron's story is far more elaborate. He says that when Jesus appeared to Joseph he gave him 'a great and precious vessel' – the Grail – that would bestow lasting joy upon all who saw it. Joseph was told that there would be only two guardians of the Grail besides himself.

Free from prison, Joseph joined his sister, Enygeus, and her husband Bron, and other Jewish converts to Christianity and they left Palestine. Some years later the children of

Enygeus and Bron set out from an unspecified place 'for the far West', to preach the word of Christ. A man named Peter, about whom we know little, also left this place to go to the 'vales of Avaron' – almost certainly Avalon – to await the third keeper of the Grail, the identity of whom is uncertain. Peter was followed by Bron, the second keeper. Joseph was left behind. Robert de Boron's story explains how the Grail passed from Palestine to 'the far West' and makes it abundantly clear that it is a Christian relic, yet it remains completely separate from the Church.

An ancient heresy

Here is a curious feature of the Grail stories. The Grail shunned and was shunned by the Church. It was not guarded by the Church, but by an independent line of Grail keepers who derived their authority directly from Jesus. And whatever bounty is received by contact with the Grail and whatever miracle is to accompany the third and final Grail keeper, it is achieved through profoundly mysterious means that have nothing to do with the teachings of the Church. It is for this reason perhaps that many people have sought to find and reveal an organised heresy concealed in the Grail legend. But if it exists it is concealed very well indeed.

About the same time as de Boron was writing, Wolfram von Eschenbach, the greatest of the German narrative poets, was working on *Parzival*, a retelling of Chrétien de Troyes's unfinished Grail story. Wolfram claims to have obtained the story from a Provençal poet named Kyot, who is said to have found the story of the Grail written in Arabic, at Toledo, Spain. Wolfram has the Grail held at the castle of Munsalvaesche and guarded by an order of chaste knights called Templeisen – almost certainly a reference to the Knights Templar.

Founded about 1118 and originally comprising nine knights whose purpose was to safeguard pilgrims to Jerusalem, the Templars professed poverty, humility and chastity, but they soon acquired vast wealth and

Above: Sir Edward Burne-Jones's *The attainment* shows a romanticised Sir Galahad venerating the Grail

Right: illustrations from the 13th-century German tale *Parzival* by Wolfram von Eschenbach. This was a retelling of Chrétien de Troyes's Grail story and has the German hero Parzival as a central figure at Arthur's court (top panel)

Below: the Ace of Cups, from the Müller Tarot pack. The origin of the meaning of the cards is obscure, but they seem to carry a profound, archetypal symbolism; this card is thought to represent the highest spiritual achievement – as does the attainment of the Holy Grail

influence. Like most religious sects, they had their own ceremonies, about which we know virtually nothing but that eventually brought about their downfall when kings, fearful of the Templars' power, accused them of heresy. The order was destroyed amid considerable bloodletting and terrible torture.

The Templars influenced or were influenced by the Cistercian monks. The Cistercian order was born in 1098 in the great movement of monastic reform that swept France during the 11th century and the greatest among those who embraced it was St Bernard, Abbot of Clairvaux, a great admirer of the Templars.

The beliefs of the Cistercians clearly influenced the anonymous author of the *Queste del Saint Graal* in the Vulgate cycle of Arthurian romances, possibly the most influential of the Grail stories. It is not a romance but a religious polemic and it introduces the purer-than-pure Galahad as an

Arthurian knight. Crammed with sententious piety, it is obsessed with chastity. It gives a list of virtues in order of merit: virginity, humility and patience – three attributes not hitherto considered to be among the many virtues of the Knights of the Round Table. Sickly Galahad seeks and finds the Holy Grail at the castle of Corbonec and is entrusted to take it to the city of Sarras, the centre of paganism until it was converted by Joseph of Arimathea. There Galahad becomes king, reigns for one year and dies.

A great marvel followed immediately on Galahad's death: the two remaining companions saw quite plainly a hand come down from heaven, but not the body it belonged to. It proceeded straight to the Holy Vessel and took both it and the lance, and carried them up to heaven, to the end that no man since has ever dared to say he saw the Holy Grail.

Although the Grail was taken away from the eyes of men, a tradition evolved that it was hidden at Glastonbury. None of the romances locates the sacred relic there, but tradition had long identified Glastonbury with Avalon and it is to 'the vales of Avaron' that Robert de Boron has Peter, the disciple of Joseph of Arimathea, go to preach the Gospel, followed by Bron the Grail Keeper. Another writer, the unknown author of *Le haut livre du Graal: Perlesvaus* ('The high book of the Grail: Perlesvaus'), dated around 1210, claimed to have translated his story from a book in Latin held by the monks at Glastonbury Abbey.

There is a tradition that the apostle Philip preached in France soon after the Crucifixion and in the 13th century the Glastonbury monks claimed that he had sent 12 disciples to Britain, led by Joseph of Arimathea. They had built the old church – a wattle and daub building that stood in the grounds of what became the abbey and that

Below: the ruins of Glastonbury Abbey, widely believed to stand on the site of an ancient wattle and daub church that was built by a group of monks who were led by Joseph of Arimathea

Bottom: the ecstasy of the saintly Sir Galahad and his companions as he receives the sacrament from the Holy Grail at the end of his long and perilous quest

was destroyed in a disastrous fire in 1184 – and then they died. The Glastonbury site remained disused until the arrival of hermits sent to England years later by Pope Eleutherius who founded the monastic community there. It is tempting to think that this story was based on a factual event concerning an early visit to these islands by Christian missionaries. But while the Glastonbury monks never laid claim to possession of the Holy Grail, their sanction of Joseph of Arimathea's presence at Glastonbury was enough to fuel a popular legend concerning a tree that rooted from Joseph's staff.

A modern elaboration of this legend is that Joseph of Arimathea was the uncle of Jesus. This notion gained ready acceptance and is often passed off as fact. A further variant is

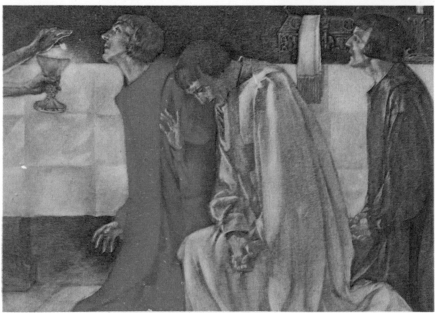

that Joseph dispatched Jesus to Britain to learn the tin trade, hence the paucity of information in the New Testament about Jesus's early life. Jesus himself is, according to this legend, supposed to have built the wattle and daub building at Glastonbury – a pleasing but improbable idea.

However, somewhere in the mists on the edge of recorded history, in the pagan beliefs of the early inhabitants of Britain, a vessel with supernatural attributes may, indeed, have played a significant role. As the pagan gods and all that was associated with them evolved into mythological heroes, so the magic vessel became a cauldron imbued with special powers. This in turn was adopted by medieval writers and became the Holy Grail, a wonderful, perplexing and haunting legend.

Who was the real King Arthur?

King Arthur's legendary exploits have all the trappings of complete fiction – but there is some evidence to show that there actually was a great British leader called Arthur who led his people to an unforgettable victory.

MERLIN THE MAGICIAN, the powerful sword Excalibur, the young Arthur fated to become not just king, but mystical hero of a 'once and future' Britain, the gallantry of the knights of the Round Table, and the Sun setting over the mysterious Isle of Avalon where the dying Arthur drifts in a gilded boat . . . The elements of the greatest British legend merge in the collective unconsciousness until the story of King Arthur seems no more than a vivid dream. Yet, as many modern researchers have discovered, it seems likely that there really was an historical Arthur. But who was he?

He was most certainly *not* a medieval knight, although his popular image today owes almost everything to that era. Yet such evidence as there is points to his having been a warrior chieftain active in the century after the collapse of Roman Britain.

It was a deeply disturbing time for the Britons. By 410 they had enjoyed nearly 400 years of unprecedented prosperity as part of the great Roman Empire, benefiting from its strong central government, the protection of a trained and efficient army and the delights of a hitherto undreamed-of civilisation. But by the late fourth century the power of Rome had begun to weaken and by 410 Emperor Honorius had enough trouble containing threats to Rome itself. He told the Britons to look to their own defences, no doubt intending that this should be only a temporary measure. As it turned out, Britain was never to belong to Rome again.

With the relatively sudden retreat of *pax romana* the British Isles became once again prey to uprisings of small bands of warring tribesmen, led by local despots. However, in 425 a dictator called Vortigern managed to assume absolute power, ruthlessly putting down any opposition and hiring an army of Anglo-Saxon mercenaries led by two continental soldiers of fortune named Hengist and Horsa. But in 455 the mercenaries rebelled and riots spread throughout the country. Vortigern's regime collapsed.

To add to the ensuing chaos, the foreign mercenaries now began attacking their former British allies. In the face of a national threat the British rallied under the banner of an enigmatic figure about whom we know little, Ambrosius Aurelianus. But about the

Arthur and a list of his conquered kingdoms, from Peter of Langtoft's *Chronicle of England* (c.1300). On his shield Arthur carries a representation of the Virgin and child, symbol of his exalted Christian ideals. The 30 kingdoms named here were never remotely connected with the historical Arthur, but Peter of Langtoft was less concerned with the truth than with creating a British hero comparable to Charlemagne

year 500 the British victories culminated in the great battle of Badon, which was said to be decisive enough to ensure peace in the land for 50 years afterwards. The hero who brought about this momentous victory was called Arthur.

Yet almost everything we know of the historical Arthur is derived from just three documents written either by his near contemporaries or in the succeeding 200 years. These documents exist today only in medieval copies – of copies.

Of course repeated copying has its pitfalls, especially when the text is written in an inflected language such as Latin, where one slip in transcription can totally alter the meaning. Besides, there is the possibility of missing out whole chunks of text or giving in to the temptation to embellish the stories – a common medieval failing. By the 10th century Arthur had become a folk hero about whom there was a complex collection of stories – most of which were fictitious. It seems likely that the scribe, seeing an obscure or cryptic reference to Arthur (or to somebody he thought was Arthur), could have added spurious information to what is otherwise an historically accurate document.

Badon and after

The earliest Arthurian document is the *De Excidio et Conquestu Britanniae* ('Concerning the ruin and conquest of Britain'), written by a monk named Gildas some time after the battle of Badon and possibly during Arthur's lifetime. It is not a formal history, but more a diatribe directed at five contemporary kings whose sinful ways Gildas believed would bring destruction to the nation in the same way as disaster had been brought by the godless and ineffectual rulers of the past. To illustrate his point, Gildas recorded the very worst features of British history, often twisting fact beyond recognition to suit his purposes.

Gildas, frugal with the names of people and places, says of the Britons under the leadership of Ambrosius:

... by God's aid, victory came to them. From that time forth, sometimes the Britons were victorious, sometimes the enemy, up to the year of the siege of Mount Badon, which was almost the last but not the least slaughter of the gallows-crew [the Saxons].

Gildas does not tell us much, but the fact that he mentions Badon – a British victory – in a book designed to illustrate the failings of, and defeats suffered by, the Britons points to the reality of the event and suggests that it was too fresh in the nation's memory for him to attempt to misrepresent it.

The *Annales Cambriae* ('Welsh annals') are a set of Easter annals – a device used by the monks to help with the complicated task of dating Easter, which is a movable feast – primarily concerned with Welsh affairs. The

Top: the Romans leave Britain in AD 410. Soon after their departure, Britain became prey to incursions by the Saxons. In this perilous time a warrior called Arthur arose – whose name, over 1500 years later, is still synonymous with victory over the invaders

Above: the Roman Emperor Honorius, whose decision it was to abandon Britain

Left: the death of the Saxon leader Hengist and the destruction of his army by Arthur at Badon. This victory was so conclusive that it was followed by 50 years of peace

pages of the Easter Annals had a wide margin in which it was the custom to make a brief entry of important events against the appropriate year (their dates are, however, unreliable). Of Arthur they say:

*c.*518 Battle of Badon in which Arthur carried the cross of Our Lord Jesus Christ on his shoulders for three days and three nights and the Britons were victors.

The old Welsh word *scuid* ('shoulder') is very similar to *scuit* ('shield'). This entry probably means that Arthur carried a representation of the cross on his shield and that the battle raged for three days. This possible error in transcription indicates that the scribe was probably copying from an early Welsh source now lost. Another entry reads: '*c.*539 the strife of Camlann in which Arthur and Mordred perished. And there was a plague in Britain and Ireland.'

The third Arthurian document is the *Historia Britonnum* ('History of the Britons'), which used to be ascribed to a monk named Nennius. It exists today as a medieval copy of the original, which was written in about the year 850. The entry that mentions Arthur by name reads:

In that time the Saxons strengthened in multitude and grew in Britain. On the death of Hengist, however, Octha, his son, passed from the northern part of Britain to the region of the Cantii [Kent] and from him arise the kings of the Cantii.

Then Arthur fought against them in those days [there follows a list of 12

Right: a medieval illustration of Merlin building Stonehenge

Below: the enigmatic monoliths of the stone circles of Stonehenge, Salisbury Plain, Wiltshire

A monument to Merlin

Stonehenge is rarely, if ever, associated with the Arthurian legends, and strictly speaking it is not an Arthurian site. But in Geoffrey of Monmouth's *Historia*, Merlin is credited with bringing the stones from Ireland by sea and erecting them on Salisbury Plain as a memorial to the Britons who died fighting the Saxons. Three elements of this story are essentially correct: the so-called bluestones are of 'foreign' origin; they were transported to Salisbury Plain by water, and Stonehenge was used as a burial site.

The outer ring of Stonehenge is made up of sarsen stones – 'sarsen' being defined as 'a boulder carried by ice in a glacial period' and possibly derived from *Saracen*, originally a name for the Muslim people of Arabia, but used later by Europeans to describe Muslims in general.

Interestingly, the Matter of Britain connects the Saracens with the 'city of Sarras'. It was to this semi-mythical place that Galahad was entrusted to take the Holy Grail; but Sarras is identified in the Arthurian legends as 'Jerusalem' – a Jerusalem that is in Britain.

battles] and in all battles he was victor. It is to be assumed that Arthur fought against the Cantii and Octha, but the separate paragraphs may suggest that these were different campaigns. Hengist's son was called Oisc (or Aesc) and he became king in 488. He died in 512 and was succeeded by his son, Octha. If Nennius really means that Arthur fought against Octha, the approximate date of 518 given in the *Annales Cambriae* for the battle of Badon could be correct.

To these documents we can add the *Anglo-Saxon Chronicle*, a remarkable document that purports to describe events from the Anglo-Saxon point of view and, as might therefore be expected, does not mention the British hero Arthur or his triumph at Badon. But strangely it also fails to record a significant *Saxon* victory between 514 and 552.

Many lengthy and complicated arguments have raged over the content of these documents, but in the final analysis it has to be admitted that, although Badon has been reasonably well-established as an historical event, there is no good reason other than tradition to link Arthur with it. So who was this Arthur around whom the legends grew?

One theory is that Arthur was an insignificant warrior fighting on the Scottish borders who was plucked from obscurity by the Britons when they needed the psychological boost of a national hero. Some of the

An illustrated page from an anonymous 15th-century *Chronicle of England*, showing a fictitious Arthur bearing his heraldic shield

battles reputedly fought by Arthur have, it is true, been located in the Border areas, but this does not explain why the legend has become so strongly linked with Wales and the West Country.

Another possibility is that the significance of Badon became apparent only 50 years later, when the Anglo-Saxons ruled Britain and the defeated Britons had been driven into Wales, Cornwall and Brittany. There they dreamed of a man who would one day lead them to final, glorious victory over their Saxon oppressors. Arthur, victor of Badon, was the prime candidate for this timeless hero.

A third reason for the lack of information about the real Arthur is suggested by references to him in several saints' *Lives*. Historically unreliable, taken as a whole they give a curiously coherent picture of Arthur that is quite different from our expectations.

The *Life of St Cadoc* (composed around the year 1100) portrays Arthur as lustful and perverse. The *Life of St Padern* speaks contemptuously of 'a certain *tyrannus* [tyrant] named Arthur'. The *Life of St Gildas* describes Arthur as a tyrannus and as a *Rex Rebellus* (a revolutionary – by implication an upstart).

It seems that the Church entertained a long and deeply rooted hostility towards Arthur that remained strong even in the 12th century when elsewhere he was regarded as a hero. But would such enmity have been accorded an insignificant chieftain on the Scottish borders or an obscure guerilla fighter in the West Country? It seems improbable. Arthur must have been an influential person to have earned such persistent hostility, yet he has never been accused of being in any way opposed to Christianity. So what did he do? We shall probably never know, but it seems likely that, since history was written by clerics and Arthur had offended the Church, he became the victim of ecclesiastical censorship.

Then in 1191 there occurred at Glastonbury an event that has become one of the most contentious issues in Arthurian scholarship: the exhumation of Arthur. He had long been associated with Glastonbury, which in his day was ringed by marshes – effectively making it an island. We are told that the Welsh called Glastonbury *Ynys Avallon*, meaning 'Isle of Apples', and it was to 'Avalon' that Arthur was taken, mortally wounded, after the battle of Camlann.

We have four accounts of the exhumation of Arthur. They differ in details but agree on two points: Arthur's grave was found between two stone pyramids – a detailed history of Glastonbury written between 1129 and 1139 by William Malmesbury tells us that these were in fact standing crosses in the ancient cemetery south of the Lady Chapel – and that in or beneath the 'coffin' there was a cross inscribed with the words: HIC IACET

Right: the archaeologist Dr Ralegh Radford who excavated the traditional site of Arthur's grave at Glastonbury Abbey in 1962. He is indicating the site of the exhumation made in 1191 by the monks – but was the grave they uncovered that of Arthur?

Above: the cross, now lost, that was said to mark Arthur and Guinevere's grave at Glastonbury

Left: a page from an early 11th-century manuscript of the *Annales Cambriae* ('Welsh Annals'). The right-hand column records the battle of Badon and the left-hand one ends with the death of Arthur and Mordred at the battle of Camlann

SEPULTUS INCLITUS REX ARTHURUS CUM WENNEVERIA UXORE SUA SECUNDA IN INSULA AVALLONIS (Here lies the famous King Arthur, with Guinevere his second wife, buried in the Isle of Avalon).

The cross can be traced down to the 18th century, when it was known to be in the nearby town of Wells, but it subsequently disappeared. A reproduction contained in the sixth edition of Camden's *Britannia* may be an accurate representation of the original; if so, an epigraphic dating of the lettering shows that the cross is not of the sixth century, when Arthur died, nor of the 12th century, when the grave was exhumed, but of the 10th century.

We know that in the 10th century Bishop Dunstan raised the level of the cemetery and enclosed it with a wall. It is therefore possible that Arthur's grave was found during the process of this work and the memorial erected above the grave removed, the lead cross being placed in the grave as identification.

In 1962 archaeologists excavated the area where Arthur's grave was said to be located and they found evidence of a pit from which a stone memorial could have been removed, and a large hole that had been dug out and refilled at some time between 1180 and 1191. This evidence is almost concrete proof that the monks of Glastonbury did exhume someone's grave in 1191. But was it the grave of Arthur?

The general opinion is that the monks perpetrated a hoax. Several motives have been suggested for their having done so, but none of the motives actually precludes the possibility that the grave really was Arthur's.

Whether Arthur existed or not will probably remain a mystery, but belief in his existence has created a potent image that transcends mere history: the fascination with the Arthurian legend will remain, and his memory will endure.

In many parts of the world civilisations that flourished for centuries have left only meagre traces to baffle the historian. BRENDA RALPH LEWIS gives an account of two vanished African societies

'THE DARK CONTINENT' was a phrase coined by Europeans to suggest not only their ignorance about the interior of Africa and its past but also a belief that there was no civilisation worth knowing about, nor any history deserving the name. The darkness was not, they believed, due to the myopia of outsiders, but was a gloom that shrouded the minds of the continent's peoples, sunk in barbarism, idolatry and poverty since time immemorial.

In large measure this view of the African past was able to persist because a continuous history of events and personalities of the kind that existed in literate Europe had not been recorded in Africa, except in those areas that became Muslim. No written accounts survive from ancient African societies. The inscriptions on stone that provide archaeologists with much valuable information elsewhere are lacking in Africa south of the Sudan. To compound the lack, the ancient Egyptians had little to say about Africa beyond the Nile.

The African archaeological record is also scanty and distorted. It is impossible to say how much evidence has been destroyed at ancient sites by those natural enemies of historical knowledge, the legions of insects and relentlessly erosive climates.

Another factor responsible for the obscurity of ancient African history may be the virulent diseases of the continent. It proved impossible in most of Africa south of the Nile

Above: an African view of European explorers. Two Portuguese seamen are shown in this 16th-century bronze from Nigeria

to rear draught animals that were resistant to disease, except in Ethiopia, where the healthy highland climate permitted the breeding of horses. In the rest of the continent, the absence of draught animals denied ancient Africans the use of the plough, and that, in turn, denied them a settled, prosperous agriculture. Many were forced to move on constantly, seeking new and better pastures. As always when life is little more than a struggle for survival, they left little or no trace of their passing, and had no chance to develop writing.

Empires of Africa

Yet despite these obstacles, some regions did develop rich and settled societies. Powerful empires arose, extending over vast areas; they flourished and declined, unknown to the chroniclers of Europe. Trade routes stretched across forests and deserts to the coasts and the continents beyond. Even evidence of contact between Africa and China has been found in the form of Chinese-made objects unearthed in East Africa. African slaves were owned by rich Cantonese in the 12th century.

From West Africa, Muslim travellers in medieval times sent reports of the rich state of Ghana, known to them as the 'land of gold'. Later the kingdom of Mali flourished, where the Muslims described their shock at seeing women and girls go naked in public.

In the 16th century the Portuguese established trading posts on the East African coast, after pioneering the sea route from

Most of the tombs of the Kushite kings, in the period when Meroë had become its capital, were built on a ridge above the city (inset). This superbly preserved example (left) shows the influence of the more ancient and far more grandiose Egyptian models

Africa's secret cities

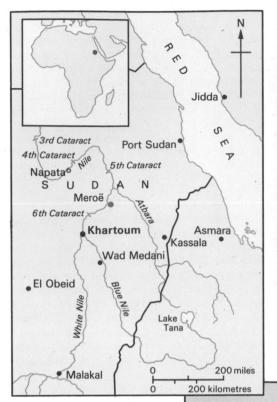

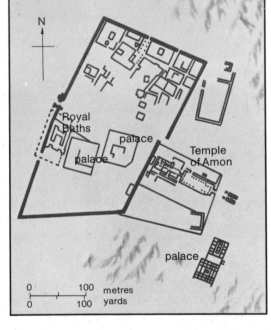

Above: Napata, capital of Kush during the period of the kingdom's greatness, and Meroë, the later capital, both lay on the Nile in what is now Sudan

Above right: ruins of one of the several temples below the hill of Barkal, at Napata. This city – really a grouping of towns – was sacked by the Egyptians in 590 BC. Although Meroë was henceforth the capital of Kush, Napata continued as a religious centre, and Kushite kings were still buried there. A number of them are represented on this stela, or inscribed slab (inset)

Right: the ground plan of ancient Meroë, imperfectly known from modern excavations. In its prime the temple of Amon was bright with colours, painted on the white stucco covering pillars, walls and altars. The baths were copies of Roman originals. Some distance to the east of Meroë lay several cemeteries, groups of royal pyramid tombs, and yet more temples

Europe to India around the Cape of Good Hope. They reported kingdoms such as the kingdom of Kongo in the area around the great lakes of East Africa.

Many of the kingdoms reported by the Portuguese proved transitory, possibly through lack of resources or the limited power of their rulers. It is impossible to say how many of them had broken up and disappeared by the time Africa was effectively penetrated by European explorers.

The gaps in African history have been imperfectly filled by dramatic oral traditions, liberally laced with many colourful myths and legends. One instance is a story from Ghana. This asserts that in about 1680, when the Ashanti chief Osei Tutu determined to unite his people against their powerful neighbour Denkera, his minister-priest Anokye caused a golden stool, henceforth to be the sacred symbol of Ashanti unity, to descend from the sky and come to rest on Osei's knees. Legends such as this, which give a magical cast to events and politics, tend to stand in the way of historical assessment, much as the legends of King Arthur once obscured understanding of the history of Britain in the period immediately following the end of Roman rule about AD 426.

Another adverse factor has been that in Africa, as in pre-Columbian America, the bulk of the best-attested early evidence has been provided by outsiders. Perhaps inevitably, many of these observers have come in from the outside equipped with their own prejudices. The 'scandal' of the naked girls of Mali, as seen through puritan Muslim eyes, is only one example.

The kingdom of Kush
An African kingdom that escaped the usual prejudices of European historians was Kush. Its cities were built in sandstone, which, though now crumbling, lasted much better than the wood, clay and straw structures of most African societies. Its language was written in two scripts, one formal and hieroglyphic, the other informal and cursive. They have yet to give up all their secrets to linguists. Most importantly, from the point of view of traditional archaeology, Kush was in close relationship with ancient Egypt, about which a great deal is known.

Kush was, so to speak, a grand-daughter of ancient Egypt. It was established by an African people who may have been of Hamitic descent, under strong Egyptian influence. Initially, it was garrisoned by Egyptians. However, by 1000 BC Kush seems to have emerged as an independent unit. Its capital at that time was Napata, just below the Fourth Cataract of the Nile. Less than three centuries later, in about 730 BC, Kush was powerful enough to sever its relationship with Egypt. The Kushite king, Piankhi, apparently aged only 20 or 21, invaded and conquered Egypt, and there founded the 25th Dynasty.

Egypt, however, was by then in a decline that the five Kushite pharaohs proved unable to halt. In fact, their dynasty lasted only about 74 years. About 656 BC the Assyrians under Assurbanipal invaded Egypt and the Kushites were ousted. In about 590 BC Kush was attacked and Napata sacked by Pharaoh Psamtik II of the succeeding, Saissan, dynasty. The Kushites were forced to move their frontier further south. At this juncture Meroë, which had been the southern administrative centre of Kush since 750 BC, became its capital. Kush subsequently became more Negroid in character and the links with Egypt and Egyptian culture began

Below: a stool, or royal throne, of the Ashanti nation of West Africa. This forest empire extended over a large area of the modern republic of Ghana. According to Ashanti legend, the first royal stool descended from the sky onto the lap of a chief who was called Osei Tutu. The Ashanti were fine metalworkers, as shown in the embellishments on the stool and in the gold ornamentation of the chief's helmet (bottom left). The skills of ironworking may have spread all over Africa from Kush, which learned them after its defeat by the Assyrians in 590 BC. Ancient slag heaps by the modern railway line at Meroë (bottom right) attest to the activity of the Kushite ironsmiths, which made Meroë the metalworking centre of Africa

specialist A. H. Sayce. A dozen iron slag heaps – piled, appropriately, on each side of the modern railway line – survive as visible evidence of this ancient industry.

It has been assumed, not unreasonably, that the techniques of ironworking spread out from Meroë to other parts of Africa, bringing them into the Iron Age. However, the routes by which ironworking was spread are still not known. There is only patchwork evidence, most of it dating from long after Meroë had fallen, some time between AD 320 and AD 350, to invaders from Axum in Ethiopia. In the northern regions of West Africa, for instance, ironworking was probably not known until after AD 500. Carbon dating puts the use of iron among peoples of East Africa between the 10th and 15th centuries. One scholar, G. A. Wainwright, suggested in 1954 that the Bantu languages of East and Central Africa may provide a clue to the spread of ironworking from Meroë to Bunyoro and from there into East Africa: in Swahili, the word for 'iron' is the Bantu word, whereas all other metals are known by Arabic names, indicating their much later introduction by the Muslims.

The spread of ironworking

Who carried the knowledge of ironworking? Mass migrations of peoples have been suggested, but largely rejected. The natural conditions of Africa inhibited movement in large numbers and it therefore seems more likely that the necessary skills were spread by craftsmen, like the small groups of smiths who still travel round Africa, crossing the borderlines between tribes.

The first scholar to visit and survey Meroë was Karl Richard Lepsius, a Prussian Egyptologist who explored the area from Khartoum to Syria between 1844 and 1845. Excavations, however, did not commence until early this century. Between 1909 and 1914, the British archaeologist John Garstang revealed evidence of Roman influence in Meroë, in the town proper and in the Sun temple on the nearby plain. The antiquity of Meroë is attested by this temple, which was described in the fifth century BC by the Greek writer Herodotus. The Egyptologist G. A.

to weaken as contacts ceased.

The disastrous clash with the Assyrians, whose iron weapons completely outclassed the Kushites' bronze, may have been among the influences that led to the development of large-scale ironworking at Meroë. Fortuitously, the site provided a plentiful supply of iron ore in the surrounding hills, and timber for smelting furnaces. The smelting process was learned from the Assyrians. The earliest ironworking tools found so far at Meroë come from the tomb of the Kushite king Harsiotef and date from about 400 BC. In time, Meroë became the metalworking centre of Africa – its Birmingham, in the phrase of the early 20th-century Assyrian

Reisner excavated Meroë's cemeteries and three groups of pyramids, between 1921 and 1923.

The chief features of Meroë, apart from its iron slag heaps, are the quay on the Nile, several palaces, a large temple to the Egyptian god Amon, the equivalent of the Greek Zeus, and a copy of a Roman bath. The work could be crude: some walls consisted only of two outer skins of dressed stone, the gap between being filled with rubble.

Reisner's work on the pyramid tombs at Meroë and at the previous capital, Napata, has yielded the names of 60 Kushite rulers. However, the latest known narrative of a ruler of Meroë comes from outside evidence – an inscription at Philae, in Egypt, which tells of an embassy sent by the Kushite king Tekeridaemani in AD 253.

This is, in fact, one of the very few dates in the history of Meroë that have been fixed. Much of the city still remains to be excavated. The chronology of Meroë, how the state was ruled and run, the precise order of the reigns of its kings and queens – these are unknown.

Light may be thrown on these questions as the Meroitic script is progressively deciphered. It is not a total puzzle: the alphabet is known to contain 17 signs for consonants and four for vowels, for example. Certain Egyptian hieroglyphic signs have been identified among the Meroitic signs, in slightly altered form. These have permitted the corresponding approximate sounds to be identified. Nevertheless, this has not been enough to make the language of Meroë fully translatable, nor to tie it in with any family of present-day African tongues. The language of Kush is another of the mysteries that hang

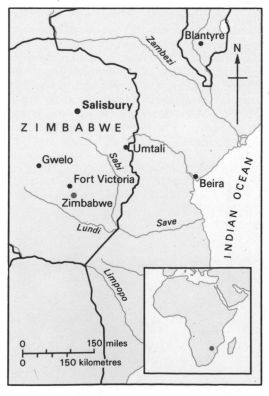

over the vanished kingdom that in its prime could master Egypt.

Far to the south, a millennium later, another African culture also built enduring monuments in stone. But the arrogant presumption of the first foreigners to study Great Zimbabwe refused to acknowledge that this royal city could be the work of a native culture.

The first non-African in modern times to see Zimbabwe was an American hunter-prospector, Adam Renders, who visited the site in 1868 and returned there in 1871 with Karl Mauch, a German schoolteacher and geologist. Renders and Mauch were astonished by the massive size of Great Zimbabwe, which is situated in the south-east of the modern state of Zimbabwe. Its Great Enclosure is over 800 feet (240 metres) in circumference, 292 feet (90 metres) long and 220 feet (67 metres) broad. It consists of roughly circular double walls, some of which are over 30 feet (9 metres) high and 14 feet (4.5 metres) wide, with large coping stones protecting the top. Inside the enclosure is a conical tower built of solid granite bricks, which stands before the court of a temple. The temple itself is oval and its walls are decorated with a frieze of delicate chevrons.

Who built Zimbabwe?

Arguably the most remarkable feature of this impressive complex, which also includes a labyrinth of staircases, courts and monoliths, was the nature of its stonework. It was made of dry masonry, with stones shaped and fitted together without mortar, but with marvellous accuracy – a method used with equal skill by the Inca builders of Peru.

Karl Mauch, who recorded the first archaeological description of Great Zimbabwe, was convinced, as was Adam Renders, that no Africans could possibly have built anything so elaborate. It must have been the work of more obviously 'civilised', probably

Above: the Great Enclosure at Zimbabwe, built on a valley floor

Left: Zimbabwe was well-placed for trade with the interior and with peoples across the Indian Ocean

Right: the scattering of ruins at Zimbabwe. Stone buildings here date from the 11th century

Below: the walls and towers of the Acropolis dominate the surrounding area

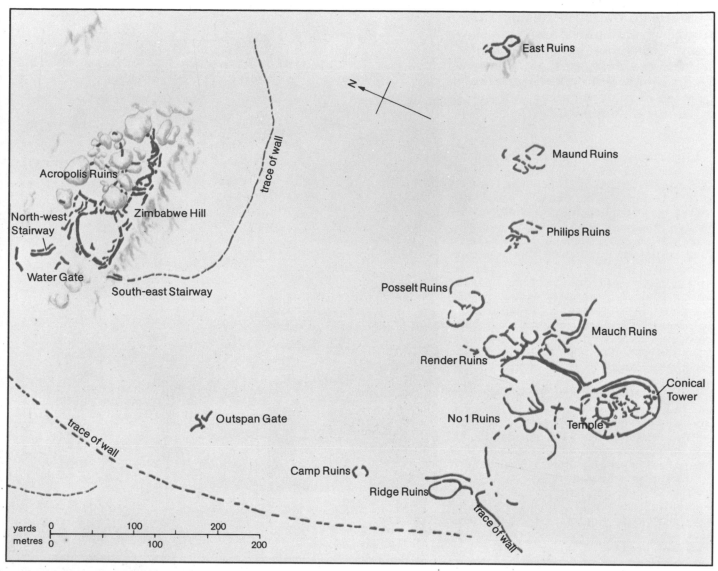

East Ruins

Maund Ruins

Philips Ruins

Acropolis Ruins

North-west Stairway

Zimbabwe Hill

Water Gate

South-east Stairway

Posselt Ruins

Mauch Ruins

Render Ruins

Conical Tower

Outspan Gate

No 1 Ruins

Temple

Camp Ruins

Ridge Ruins

trace of wall

trace of wall

trace of wall

| yards | 0 | 100 | 200 | |
| metres | 0 | 100 | 200 | |

white-skinned, architects. Among the candidates were a long-vanished white race of Africa, and the fortress builders of King Solomon. Others were Phoenicians – especially favoured by Karl Mauch – or the architects of the Queen of Sheba. Mauch thought that the temple of Great Zimbabwe might well be a copy of King Solomon's palace, where the Queen of Sheba was a guest, and that the complex itself was the capital of gold-rich Ophir, a biblical El Dorado, which the book of Genesis places somewhere in the region of Arabia.

In formulating these theories, now recognised as ridiculous, Renders and Mauch observed the conditions of the local Makalanga people, not much above those of the Stone Age, and assumed that they had always lived like that. What they did not take into account, when reasoning thus, was the well-known pattern of rise and decline of civilisations. The Makalanga, the 19th-century descendants of the advanced society that had built Zimbabwe, had reverted to a more primitive cultural level.

More knowledgeable and less arrogant archaeologists have since established that the 'long-vanished race' that built Great Zimbabwe was more likely to have been black than white or Semitic. Zimbabwe was, in fact, only part of a larger culture, named Azanian, which also dug canals, built wells and worked gold mines. This Azanian state has left behind these, the only large ancient stone buildings in southern Africa, and its gold probably enabled it to prosper for some 300 years, until about AD 1500. From around 1400, Great Zimbabwe appears to have been a royal capital, a ceremonial centre for worship and the repository of the royal tombs. Zimbabwe's earliest structures date from the eighth century and the splendid edifices that so impressed Mauch and Renders date from the 16th and 17th. Great Zimbabwe survived the Azanian state by more than 300 years. It succumbed to the depredations of African invaders, probably Zulus, in about 1830. After that, Zimbabwe's fame faded quickly: no memory of it survived when the first Europeans came upon it 50 years later.

At Mohenjo-Daro in Pakistan and Angkor in Kampuchea are the magnificent remains of two of the world's greatest, most vigorous civilisations. Both cities were the centres of huge empires that suddenly disappeared. Why?

If these stones c

CIVILISATIONS THAT 'VANISH' leave behind titillating traces of their existence. History suggests the process of extinction is gradual, if only because the numbers of people involved may be quite large. In addition, the natural human tendency in the face of disaster is to hang on to home and possessions as long as possible, and leave only when no alternative exists.

The force most likely to bring about an abrupt exodus is invasion and conquest. This was certainly involved in the 'disappearance' of the people of Angkor, capital of the Khmer empire of Indochina, and may also have accounted for the end of the Indus Valley civilisation, which was centred on the cities of Mohenjo-Daro and Harappa.

Of the two civilisations, less is known of the Indus Valley, owing chiefly to the great antiquity of the site. Dating from about 2500 BC, it is classed, after Mesopotamia, China and Egypt, among the world's earliest civilisations, and saw the beginnings of agriculture in the Indian subcontinent.

The wars that may have brought about the end of the Indus civilisation about 1750 BC may have been reinforced by other destructive factors. The aggressors in this case may have been the Aryans, who were entering India from the north from about 2000 BC. In the Indus Valley, at the cities of Mohenjo-Daro and Harappa and some 40 other sites, the Aryans found a highly organised, productive and widespread civilisation. Like the Khmers at Angkor, the Indus Valley people based their life and prosperity on an elaborate drainage and irrigation system. The irrigation channels and dams like the two cities themselves, were built of long-lasting baked brick. A significant pointer to the power and extent of this civilisation is that brick sizes were standard not only in Mohenjo-Daro and Harappa, which lie about 400 miles (650 kilometres) apart, but also in places along the tributaries of the River Ganges in the east, right down to the south coast of India. Standardised weights and measures also existed, indicating that some central government had jurisdiction over this vast area.

The civilisation appears to have been sophisticated. There was a complex sanitation system, in which each house was connected to a network of brick-lined sewers. The two cities were obviously the products of tidy minds, for they were laid out in a regular grid pattern, with main streets running north-south and minor roads running

Right: a map of the Indus Valley. Here, more than 4000 years ago, there flourished a highly developed civilisation – classed, after Mesopotamia, China and Egypt, as one of the world's oldest. It suddenly came to an end around 1750 BC – for reasons that are a mystery

Below: a plan of the once magnificent city of Harappa

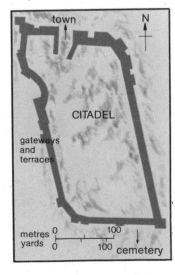

east-west. The potter's wheel was in use here, and cotton was grown. The population of each city is reckoned to have been about 35,000. This points to a degree of prosperity, which was partly founded on trade, not only in the Indus Valley itself, but abroad.

Traces of Indus Valley trade goods have been found, in fact, as far away as the Persian Gulf. Voyages of such distances were probably made hugging the coast, but the venture nonetheless indicates a high degree of enterprise and seamanship. The vessels that

ld speak

Left: the ruins of the city of Mohenjo-Daro – twin centre, with Harappa, of the ancient Indus Valley civilisation

Below: a site plan of Mohenjo-Daro, showing the great public buildings of the citadel – the *stupa*, or temple, the granary, baths and assembly hall – and parts of the residential quarter with its complex system of streets

possessed bronze weapons, which could have done the damage found on some of the skeletons. The Indus peoples had no metals, which put them at a severe disadvantage in battle. Nevertheless, superiority of weapons is not always a deciding factor in war, and other archaeological evidence suggests that the invaders fell upon a city already in the process of decline.

Both Mohenjo-Daro and Harappa were provided with defence systems, in strongly fortified citadels with watch towers. However, some scholars believe that certain less well-ordered and well-constructed buildings found on the sites may indicate there was a weakening of the central government, and therefore of the organisation of defence. At this time, too, the Indus civilisation may have been hastened to its end by deforestation, with consequent erosion and desiccation of the soil. The baking of bricks for the building of the Indus cities involved fuelling the brick ovens with large numbers of trees. By about 1750 BC, after some 750 years of habitation, it may be that this process went too far. It is now well-known that reducing the number of trees below a certain point impairs the fertility of the soil and, with that, the size of agricultural yield. If this, indeed, occurred in the Indus Valley, it would not be the first or the last time that human beings have committed ecological suicide.

A failure to manage natural resources may also have played a part in the mysterious eclipse of the medieval Cambodian society of

conducted this trade must have used the brick-lined dock at Lothal, 450 miles (720 kilometres) south-east of Mohenjo-Daro, at the head of the Gulf of Cambay now in India's Gujarat State. The Lothal dock was connected by a 2½-mile (4-kilometre) channel to the Varmada River. It was some 76 feet (23 metres) long and 10½ feet (3 metres) wide. Anchor stones of large ships have been found at Lothal; so too have thousands of seals, made to stamp impressions into clay: their purpose, it seems, was to mark trade goods.

Many of the ruins, especially at Harappa, are in a dilapidated state, with much more excavation still to be done. The primitive pictographic script has yet to be deciphered. Most of our ideas about the Indus Valley civilisation are, therefore, of necessity conjectural. That, of course, includes explanations of its end. Certain evidence indicates that at Mohenjo-Daro the end came suddenly and violently. In one of the houses there, 13 skeletons of men, women and children have been found, of which two appear to have died from axe or sword blows to the head. Two more skeletons were found near a public well, and three others in a nearby lane. Nine skeletons, five of them children, were uncovered lying in contorted postures indicating death by violence.

A telling factor in this tragic tale is that the Aryans, the most often cited culprits,

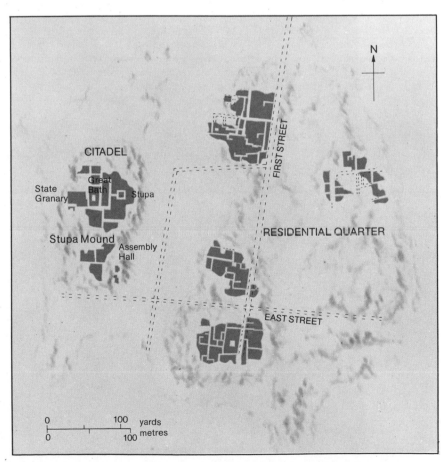

Left: this carved stone figure, found in Mohenjo-Daro, demonstrates the high level of artistic achievement of the Indus Valley civilisation

Right: one of the narrow streets of Mohenjo-Daro. Like many American cities, both Harappa and Mohenjo-Daro were designed on grid systems, with the main streets running north-south and the minor ones running east-west

Angkor. We have much more abundant and more direct evidence concerning Angkor than we have concerning the Indus Valley civilisation, but many mysteries still surround its fall.

Angkor was founded in the ninth century AD, and was a mighty, fabulously wealthy power in Indochina for some 600 years. The scale of the Khmer achievement is still evident in the ruins of Angkor. The temple of Angkor Wat, its huge towers shaped like lotus buds, still rises out of the jungle to stupefy visitors. Its size alone is overwhelming – 5000 feet (1500 metres) by 4000 feet (1200 metres). But the beauty of its terraces and pavilions, its 200-foot (60-metre) moat, filled with water lilies, lotus blossoms, wild orchids and other flowers, its vivid bas-reliefs and sculptures, are all astounding.

Below: the magnificent medieval temple of Angkor Wat, which stands, together with the neglected royal citadel of Angkor Thom, in the depths of the Kampuchean jungle (see map, below right). For 500 years after it was founded in the ninth century AD, Angkor was the centre of the mighty and fabulously rich Khmer empire. Suddenly, around the middle of the 15th century, the empire collapsed and Angkor was abandoned – leaving a mystery as great as that of the end of the Indus Valley civilisation

And around the temple are the remains of some 600 others, and beyond a stretch of jungle lie the ruins of the Khmer capital, Angkor Thom, enclosed in an 8-mile (13-kilometre) wall. Although more dilapidated than Angkor Wat, which has been kept in repair by wandering Buddhist monks ever since it was abandoned, Angkor Thom still possesses many impressive sights. They include the entrance gate and Royal Terrace, a plethora of beautiful carvings and the Elephant Terrace, carved with a quarter-mile (400-metre) procession of elephants.

Yet by the time Henri Mouhot, a French naturalist, came upon Angkor accidentally in 1861, the city was abandoned and neglected, gripped fast in the stranglehold of undergrowth and huge tree roots. What disaster had overtaken it?

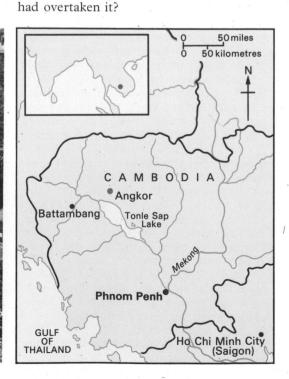

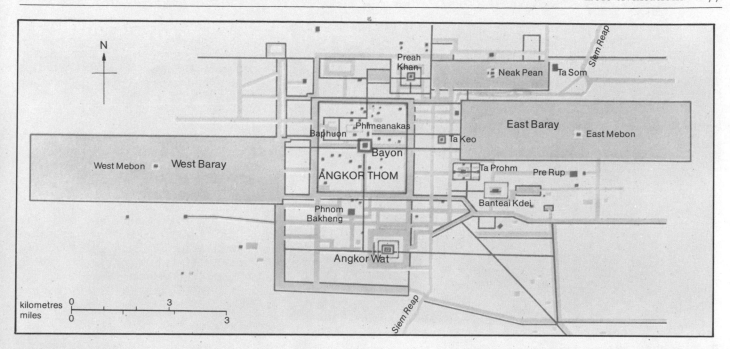

Part of the historical record is clear. Angkor fell to the warlike Siamese in 1431. The seven-month siege of Angkor and the subsequent looting, destruction and killing perpetrated by the Siamese was the last in a long series of onslaughts by these warlike neighbours of the Khmers.

However, the disaster was compounded by several other factors, which between them rendered Angkor impotent and made the city an easy target. These included blood feuds in the Khmer royal family, a shortage of rice, the weakness, through neglect, of Angkor's irrigation system, the flooding of the Mekong River, soil exhaustion and erosion and the defection of several subject states of the Khmer empire.

According to a generally accepted account, the Siamese returned to Angkor a year later, in 1432, for more rich booty, only to find the city deserted. The surviving population – reckoned to have been a million before the onslaught of 1431 – had apparently disappeared into the surrounding jungle. This

Above: a site plan of Angkor. The complex is fed by the Siem Reap River and irrigated by a system of reservoirs, or barays, and canals, that made it possible to cultivate rice all the year round. Perhaps the most striking aspect of Angkor, however, was its temples – there were over 600 of them besides Angkor Wat itself; the more important ones are named here

Below: a view of the water terraces of Angkor Wat, seen across the canal

is the great mystery that still exercises students of Khmer history.

Researches have shown an early Khmer habit of deserting cities when they became unsatisfactory. Reasons offered for their disappearance from Angkor, apart from fear of further Siamese aggression, have included a plague, a slave revolt, the crippling cost to a ruined economy of maintaining the expensive nobility and the temples, and a weakening of resolve brought about by the fatalistic, gentle teachings of Buddhism.

It was, however, no small thing for thousands of people suddenly to abandon themselves to the mercies of the surrounding jungle and its predatory animals. Nor was it easy for devout Buddhists to commit the sacrilege of deserting the temples of their faith, with their wealth of religious images.

A theory advanced by John Audric in *Angkor and the Khmer empire* (1972) takes into account the fact that these religious objections must have lost their power before despair could become strong enough to drive

Laos) and afterwards to a site near Phnom Penh, now capital of modern Kampuchea. Here, they built a royal palace with the bell-shaped spire typical of south-east Asia, sited on a mountain on which the Khmers had traditionally built temples. It is significant that Phnom Penh dates from 1434, when a king named Pohea Yat built his capital there. Audric's argument seems to be borne out.

There was, it seems, a brief return to Angkor in the 17th century by the Khmer king Barom Reachen II, but the Khmers soon returned to Phnom Penh.

Europeans were sceptical about the reports of Angkor's magnificence that were sent back by missionaries in the 17th century. In 1604 the Portuguese priest Quiroga de San Antonio came upon the city, and in 1672 a French missionary, Père Chevreuil, also reached it. One report by a Portuguese traveller described a 'forest of huge and

the Khmers from Angkor. This could not have happened in as short a time as one year, according to Audric. He suggests that the Siamese did not return in 1432: they came back after a rather longer period and the Khmer royal family remained at Angkor until about 1433, together with the Buddhist priesthood. During those two years or so, vigorous efforts were made to repair the appalling damage done by the Siamese to the irrigation system. An emergency supply of rice was provided by dry cultivation, with slash-and-burn clearing of the jungle for the planting of crops. These methods proved inadequate, however, and the problems of Angkor were further intensified by natural disasters – devastating floods and an epidemic of malaria – and a violent uprising among the Khmers' slaves. Though the rising was suppressed, the accumulated chaos and despair was too great for life at Angkor to continue.

It was then, Audric postulates, that the Khmers moved out, first to Bassac (now in

Above: a detail of the fabulously rich stone carvings that decorate every wall in Angkor – the face of the King Bakong temple

Inset: a bas-relief from the ruined citadel of Angkor Thom, showing a festival procession

terrifying ruins of palaces, halls and temples, the size of which would be unbelievable if he had not seen them.' The clearing of the site and its thorough study and restoration awaited the advent of the French colonial regime in the 19th century.

Further research may make the abandonment of Angkor seem less mysterious. It may even show that it was not as thoroughgoing an excavation as is now generally believed by scholars. Perhaps some Khmers, greatly reduced in numbers, resumed their lives there after the Siamese had finished their work of destruction in 1431.

But in the present state of our knowledge, the enigma remains. Angkor still deserves its romantic reputation as a 'lost city' – the fruit of centuries of craftsmanship, artistic genius and engineering achievement, unaccountably abandoned to be overwhelmed by the dense Cambodian jungle.

Last refuge of the Incas

When the Inca empire was finally subjugated by the Spanish, the last stronghold of its rulers was abandoned and its location forgotten. This chapter explains how, after two centuries of exploration, the lost city of the Incas may have been found

THE EMPIRE OF THE INCAS, Tahuantinsuyu (Land of the Four Quarters), was invaded by the Spanish in 1532. The triumph of the Spaniards was rapid, but not complete. They captured and executed Atahualpa, the Sapa Inca (Supreme Lord) in 1533, but his brother Manco soon initiated a revolt against the Incas' new masters. In 1537, after the failure of this rebellion, Manco fled to the village of Vilcapampa, which he built up into a stronghold. It was sacked by the Spanish in 1539, but Manco escaped and later returned to the city, which was to survive for 35 years against the attacks of the Spanish. Yet this last royal fortress of a great empire was so completely engulfed by the jungle and so thoroughly forgotten that even today we cannot be sure that we have correctly identified its remains.

Until the death of Manco in 1544 he masterminded guerrilla activity and exploited the chaos caused by struggles for power among the white invaders. Although Manco's less resolute son and heir, Sayri Tupac Inca, submitted to the Spaniards in 1557, this did nothing to diminish the will to resist at Vilcapampa. After Sayri's departure for Spanish-held Cuzco, his *llautu*, the scarlet-fringed crown of the Sapa Incas, passed to his brother Titu Cusi Yupanqui. Titu Cusi maintained his independence for

13 years by a judicious mixture of subversion and diplomacy. For example, while stirring up native revolts on the borders of Spanish-controlled Peru, he allowed missionaries into Vilcapampa and even signed a peace treaty with the Spaniards. Right up to his death in 1571, Titu Cusi kept the Spaniards hoping that he would surrender.

Viceroy Francisco de Toledo, who arrived in Peru in 1569, was not, however, a man who lived on hopes. Instead, in April 1572, Toledo declared war on Vilcapampa. Six weeks later, on 1 June, the large viceregal army defeated the new Sapa Inca, Tupac Amaru. Vilcapampa itself was occupied on 24 June, and Tupac Amaru fled deep into the forest. Toledo's forces pursued and captured him and publicly beheaded him.

This was the end of Vilcapampa, as Toledo fully intended it should be. After the death of Tupac Amaru the rain forest closed in, to engulf the royal refuge and obliterate it from maps and from local memory in a tangle

Machu Picchu (above left), most spectacular of Inca cities, was thought by its discoverer Hiram Bingham to be the most worthy site for the last refuge of the empire's hard-pressed rulers. Amid extensive terraces, it is perched high above the Urubamba River. However, it was probably never more than a supplier of crops to the city of Cuzco, the capital at the time of the Spanish invasion. It was one of a chain of mountain-top towns, linked to Cuzco by a paved road – just visible here beyond Pisac (above)

Top: after the murder of the emperor Atahualpa, his body was decapitated

of tree roots and jungle undergrowth. The silver mines established by the Spaniards after 1572 were worked out within only 40 years. By the 18th century, the former boom town near the mines, San Francisco de la Vitoria, was little more than a poor village. In 1768 the traveller Cosmé Bueno wrote that the Vilcapampa area retained 'only the memory of the retreat of the last Inca.' But the city's name, in the spelling Vilcabamba, survived in many Peruvian place-names.

Already, though, the quest for this last, lost retreat was exerting a fascination. Some time before 1768, Cosmé Bueno noted, a party of intrepid explorers had crossed the Apurimac River on rafts and struggled up some 5000 feet (1500 metres) to the spur above the right bank, on which stood the ancient town of Choqquequirau. There they found the remains of 'sumptuous houses and palaces', and great quantities of quarried stone. Choqquequirau seemed to be the

Above: Don Francisco de Toledo declared war on Vilcapampa in April 1572

asylum', in the words of the explorer Angrand. He was drawn to Choqquequirau by these rumours in 1847. His view that this was, indeed, the royal hideaway was shared by the Peruvian geographer Antonio Raimondi, who explored the surrounding valley in 1865. Raimondi offered as evidence a passage from the narrative of the Spanish priest Antonio de Calancha, written in 1639, in which Vilcapampa was put at 'two long days' march' from a place called Puquiura; this distance, according to Raimondi, encompassed Choqquequirau.

Choqquequirau continued to be regarded as the most likely site for Vilcapampa until 1909. In that year its claim faltered, after it had been thoroughly but unsuccessfully searched for treasure by the Prefect of Apurimac Province. In addition, the picture was changed in that year by documentary evidence not available to Angrand or Raimondi. The *Relación*, or report to the

Right: the Inca empire embraced modern Peru and Bolivia, together with parts of Ecuador and Chile, but its heartland was high in the Peruvian Andes. Modern exploration has uncovered countless Inca towns and villages. Machu Picchu and Choqquequirau were at different times thought to be the lost city of Vilcapampa, but today Espíritu Pampa is favoured. Part of the case rests on nearby place-names: many correspond with places passed through by the Inca ruler Manco when, in his flight, he travelled from Vitcos to Vilcapampa to mount his final resistance

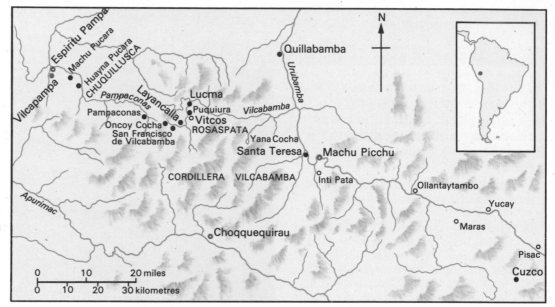

last Inca stronghold, Vilcapampa – the first of several sites to be so identified.

The most decisive evidence would have been the discovery, if possible, of treasure left behind by the Incas. Treasure was sought there in the 1820s by the local landowner, one Señor Tejada, and in 1834 by a French nobleman, the Comte de Sartiges. Neither found much evidence of the fabled Inca wealth. Sartiges did, however, see some typically Inca architecture, and also noted a record of Spanish envoys who met Sayri Tupac Inca in a town on the right bank of the Apurimac, which they had to cross in order to reach it. Sartiges assumed that Choqquequirau was the town in question and also the last retreat of the Incas, which had been called Vilcapampa erroneously.

Despite the failure of Tejada and Sartiges to locate any treasure, rumours persisted of immense riches buried among the ruins of Choqquequirau when 'the last survivors of the race of the Sun retired to this savage

Above: Inca noblemen building a city, as drawn by Guaman Poma de Ayala, the half-caste author of a narrative of Inca life

King of Spain, written by Titu Cusi in 1570, and the chronicles of Baltasar de Ocampo, published in 1610, were both discovered. On studying this new evidence, the historian Carlos Romero concluded that Choqquequirau was nothing more than an outpost of the Vilcapampa state, and that a more fruitful site in the search for the last Inca refuge was at Puquiura. Near Puquiura, Romero believed, lay the Inca town of Vitcos, which, according to Titu Cusi's *Relación*, was on the route taken to Vilcapampa by the fleeing Manco in 1537. Titu Cusi wrote that his father 'returned to the town of Vitcos, and from there went to Vilcapampa, where he remained for some days, resting. He built houses and palaces to make it his principal residence. . . .' In addition, Puquiura was also mentioned in conjunction with Vitcos by Antonio de Calancha and Baltasar de Ocampo.

In 1911 the American explorer Hiram Bingham, following clues in Calancha and

Ocampo, located and identified Vitcos. Only two weeks earlier Bingham had discovered a spectacular 'city in the sky', Machu Picchu. Superbly constructed from accurately inter-locking masonry, following the curves of the mountain on which it was perched, Machu Picchu lay above a high, sheer drop into the waters of the Urubamba River. The city was such a triumph of construction, and located in so commanding a site, that Bingham was led to identify Machu Picchu with Vilca-pampa. Like Choqquequirau, Machu Picchu was 'two long days' march' from Vitcos, as mentioned by Calancha. When cleared of its thick coat of jungle undergrowth in 1912 and 1915, the city's impressive size became apparent. Bingham was reminded of Calancha's comment that Vilcapampa was the largest city in the region.

However, the remainder of Bingham's evidence was somewhat tenuous. He con-cluded, for instance, that a hollow tube found at Machu Picchu was intended for smoking the narcotic yellow seed of the local *huilca* tree. This, he thought explained the name Vilcapampa: it meant the pampa (plain) of *huilca*.

Bingham also sought out a swampy lake, which according to Calancha was called 'Ungacacha' and lay on the route from Puquiura to Vilcapampa that was followed by Spanish friars and, later, by the Toledo military expedition of 1572. From the names of various lakes and swamps given him by local Indians, Bingham picked the one that to his ears sounded most similar – Yana Cocha – and identified it with Ungacacha.

On the strength of Bingham's great repu-tation as an explorer more than on anything else, Machu Picchu was regarded as the lost Vilcapampa for almost 50 years. A significant

Above: Hiram Bingham, the young American explorer who made the most brilliant finds in the exploration of the Inca past. In a single month in 1911, Bingham discovered the ruins at Machu Picchu, Vitcos and Espiritu Pampa

piece of evidence against it was to emerge, however, quite apart from Bingham's wish-ful thinking and suspect interpretations of place-names: Machu Picchu was refresh-ingly free from signs of looting by Spaniards and there was no evidence, either, of their having occupied it or resided there.

These facts, prompting doubts about Machu Picchu's claim to be Vilcapampa, began to emerge with the American ex-pedition that began in 1940. The expedi-tion's leader, Paul Fejos, noted that the site was not built for defence, as Vilcapampa certainly would have been. In addition, the expedition revealed that Machu Picchu was not an isolated site, but just one in a string of mountaintop towns – Pisac, Yucay, Maras, Inti Pata, Ollantaytambo – all overlooking the turbulent Urubamba River, all con-nected by a paved road, each about 10 miles (16 kilometres) from the next, all leading towards Cuzco. By their long flights of terracing Fejos judged that these sites were used to grow luxury crops especially for the Inca royal court at Cuzco in the days before the Spanish conquerors arrived.

Ollantaytambo (left) is one of the best-preserved Inca cities, inhabited today. The town proper is overlooked by a formidable citadel, within which is the Sun Temple (above). The Spanish attacked the city and one of them reported: 'When we reached Tambo we found it so well fortified that it was a horrifying sight. . . . So many men suddenly appeared on every side that every visible stretch of wall was covered in Indians.' The Spanish were driven back and escaped at night, fighting their way back to Cuzco

As a result of these investigations Machu Picchu, like Choqquequirau before it, dropped out of the contest, and the search for Vilcapampa turned back to the dense, tangled rain forest. The impenetrability of the area was such that the American expedition of 1963, which explored the hills between the Apurimac and Urubamba Rivers, was dropped by parachute. Here, in an area some 30 miles (45 kilometres) north of Espiritu Pampa, the explorers found no trace of anything resembling the Incas' retreat. However, according to present-day theories, they were tantalisingly close; so too was Hiram Bingham, who visited Espiritu Pampa briefly after discovering Vitcos.

In July 1964 another American, Gene Savoy, hacked a large area of Espiritu Pampa out of its cocoon of jungle to reveal a considerable city, with some 300 houses, 60 larger buildings, a bridge and watercourses, all of characteristic Inca construction. In the surrounding plain, traces of Inca roads were discovered, crossing the peaks of the Marcacocha–Picchacocha range, close to which lay the border between Inca and

Spanish Peru in the years of Vilcapampa's independence.

Savoy concluded that Espiritu Pampa was Vilcapampa, a view since endorsed by the explorer-author John Hemming. Hemming cites, as part of the evidence, two documentary sources undiscovered when Bingham reached Machu Picchu in 1911 and apparently not given much weight by Gene Savoy in 1964. These were a dispatch from General Martin Hurtado de Arbieto, the commander of Viceroy Toledo's army of 1572, which was published in 1935, and the first part of Martin de Murua's history of Peru from 1590 to 1611, discovered in 1945 and published in 1962. Arbieto wrote to Toledo that Vilcapampa grew sugar cane, cotton, coca – all tropical produce; Murua noted several times that Vilcapampa was in

These densely overgrown walls (left) and terraces of once-cultivated land (top) lie in the forests of Espiritu Pampa. Large areas of these ruins were cleared by an expedition led by an American, Gene Savoy (above). Are they the remains of Vilcapampa?

'hot country'. These descriptions fitted Espiritu Pampa, at its relatively low altitude of 3300 feet (1000 metres), but not Machu Picchu, perched in the mountains at three times that height. In fact, Titu Cusi wrote in his *Relación* of 1570 that Manco's 'principal residence' had a warm climate, from which Vitcos served as a retreat, 'for it is in a cold district.' In addition, Vilcapampa's plant and animal life, as detailed by Martin de Murua, and Arbieto's observation that, like Cuzco, Vilcapampa lay in a broad valley, again pointed to Espiritu Pampa.

Hemming believes, too, that 'Ungacacha', the swampy lake on the way to Vilcapampa, was more likely to have been Oncoy Cocha than Bingham's Yana Cocha. If Oncoy Cocha is the lake in question, the route Calancha described would have led the Spaniards to Espiritu Pampa, not Machu Picchu. In fact, all Calancha's place-name clues along the route to Vilcapampa indicate north-west movement from Vitcos into the valley beyond – towards Espiritu Pampa. Machu Picchu is in the opposite direction.

Vilcapampa's long survival was partly due to the extreme rigours of the surrounding terrain. In places the land soars to 13,000 feet (4000 metres) and more above sea level. Snow-capped peaks are interspersed with stiflingly hot, tangled, bat-infested jungles, which are slashed by turbulent rivers and streams, and dotted with snake-riddled swamps and quagmires. Most movement was, and still is, possible only at peril along precipitous paths flanked by yawning ravines. Small wonder that, with natural defences like these, this last royal bolt-hole of the Incas was able to withstand the assaults of the Spanish for decades – and the pryings of later explorers for centuries.

Gods from the stars?

**Beings from the sky, chariots with wings and creatures part-man and part-animal are told of in legend and depicted in art.
PETER JAMES describes the fascinating variety of what some regard as evidence of visits by aliens from space**

ACCORDING TO THE BIBLE as it is taught in Sunday schools the world over, we are all descendants of the first human couple, Adam and Eve. Though very few of us today would take the story literally, that is how we imagine the biblical myth goes. But there is a curious textual qualification to this, which is usually glossed over. Genesis also states, quite explicitly, that a *second* strain was added to the human gene-pool – a strain that was not of this world but from a 'heavenly source'. Immediately before the description

'Ancient astronaut' writers say Man did not evolve only from earthly beings like Adam and Eve (above)

Below: Vishnu rides on the bird-god Garuda

of the flood, chapter 6 of Genesis reads (in the New English Bible):

> When mankind began to increase and to spread all over the earth and daughters were born to them, the sons of the gods saw that the daughters of men were beautiful; so they took for themselves such women as they chose. . . .
> In those days, when the sons of the gods had intercourse with the daughters of men and got children by them, the Nephilim [or 'fallen ones'] were on earth. They were the heroes of old, men of reknown.

These biblical verses differ strikingly from the rest of the creation narrative and have raised many problems for translators and theologians. Who were the 'gods' involved? The Bible denies the very existence of 'other gods'. The word for 'gods' – *elohim* – can in fact be just as comfortably translated as 'God' (whose name is given a plural spelling throughout most of the creation narrative). But in that case, why do these 'sons of God' interfere in earthly affairs, when God is said to have created Adam in his likeness as

his steward on earth?

The 'sons of God' episode reads like a piece of fossil paganism that escaped the careful editing of later generations of devout Jewish scribes. It could happily smoulder as a problem of biblical exegesis were it an isolated instance. But the same strange belief in a bygone period when beings from 'heaven' would descend to take human brides, is found not only in this obscure biblical verse; it is present, for example, in the well-known Greek myths about the amorous adventures of their gods. And in classical times any noble Greek worth his salt would try to trace his ancestry through heroes and princes to one or other of the Olympian gods.

Affairs between mortals and beings from another world feature frequently in the folk-lore of the North American Indians. The Thompson Indians of British Columbia told how 'people of the sky' once stole a married woman. Outraged, all the creatures of the earth started a fruitless war against the powerful 'sky people'. To get to the sky the 'earth people' built a flimsy structure, which collapsed when the 'sky people' retaliated. Massive casualties resulted, and many kinds of animals were extinguished. In the version told by the Quinalt Indians of Washington the aggressors were said to come from the 'sky country, where the stars are'. The abduction of two maidens to the stars brought about conflict and disaster for the tribes.

Such unions did not always end in tragedy. The Maoris indirectly ascribe their civilisation to an illicit love affair between the daughter of a chief and a prince of 'the country in the sky'. The intruder was caught by the Maori chief, but then accepted as his son-in-law. A Maori deputation was allowed to visit the 'sky-country' where invaluable arts were learned from the superior beings there. Similar tales of the days when there were close ties between the beings of heaven and mankind can be found in widely separated cultures. The Machinguenga Indians of the Peruvian jungle tell of 'people of the heavens who came to earth on a shining road in the sky'. Japanese myth claims that access to the earth from the heavens was once provided by a kind of bridge, enabling the gods to pay frequent visits.

Lingering questions

What, then, are we to make of these curious, sometimes ridiculous sounding, legends about relationships between people and 'sky beings'? Orthodox anthropology has no standard explanation of such stories, in which the link with what we now term 'paranormal' phenomena is self-evident. Some of the legends recall the UFO abduction stories of our own time. And it should be noted that a proportion of claimed UFO contacts include some kind of sexual encounter with the aliens – as unlikely sounding as the supposed mixed marriages between 'gods' and the 'daughters of men' in the old legends.

Are we dealing here with some mysterious quality of the human psyche, which compels widely separated peoples to develop similar fantasies around a belief in intelligent beings superior to Man? The alternative – that these tales are vestiges of some sort of historical contact between Man and alien beings – is difficult to accept. Nevertheless, it has been argued persuasively by a number of theorists whose reasoning should not be lightly brushed aside.

One serious attempt to penetrate the tangle of myth and belief about the 'sons of God' was made by dowser T. C. (Tom) Lethbridge, one of the most colourful characters of English archaeology until his death in 1971. He had resigned in disgust in 1957 from his post as the Keeper of Anglo-Saxon

Above: *The fall of the rebel angels* by Pieter Brueghel. The fallen angels or Nephilim have been interpreted as an explanation of the origin of evil. In the Book of Enoch, written in the 2nd and 1st centuries BC, it is said that the rebellious angels were expelled from heaven and made to live on Earth, where they passed forbidden knowledge on to man

Below: This neo-Assyrian cylinder seal (950–612 BC) depicts weird creatures part-man, part-fish and part-bird. Are they aliens?

This sketch of an unexcavated figure, 100 feet (30 metres) tall, was plotted by T.C. Lethbridge from information he received after using a stainless steel bar as a dowsing-rod at Wandlebury. The number 1 indicates a metal necklace; 2 a shield; 3 could be sling-stones; 4 marks the point where an old track has destroyed the legs; and 5 is where a modern pipeline is sited. It is taken from Lethbridge's book, *A step in the dark*

Antiquities at the Cambridge Archaeology Museum. He had for long been peeved with the lack of imagination of most archaeologists, and it was the last straw when many of his colleagues rejected out of hand his claim that gigantic chalk figures of gods, along with astral symbols, lay beneath the turf of Wandlebury Camp, Cambridgeshire. Moving to Devon, Lethbridge renewed an old interest in dowsing, for which he developed refined techniques and applied them successfully in his archaeological research. His studies and writings broadened to take in ESP and other parapsychological problems, and his work culminated in a controversial study, *The legend of the sons of God*. 'As it happened,' explained Lethbridge, 'I had been interested in the problem of who were the "sons of God" for many years and had sought enlightenment from archaeologists, anthropologists and theologians at Cambridge and elsewhere without getting the slightest satisfaction. Nobody knew the answer.'

Lethbridge appreciated the scope of the problem, which touches on fundamental issues: what were gods? And why had the bulk of mankind always apparently believed that there were such things? Of course he had been given plenty of 'explanations' by academic colleagues in terms of their own pet theories, but the 'legend of the sons of God' seemed to defy analysis: 'Now how does this piece of legend fit in with any known "ism"?' asked Lethbridge. 'It is not totemism, anthropomorphism or anything of that kind. It is a definite statement of fact that a race known as the sons of God intermarried with another known as the daughters of men.'

'Remarkable flying machines'

Lethbridge drew upon other mythological evidence about the vehicles used by the ancient 'gods'. Elijah had been swept up to heaven in a fiery chariot. The Greek gods of Olympus travelled in aerial vehicles. It was not only the product of Greek imagination, he said, 'for there were Hindu stories, too, of godlike personages who actually had remarkable flying machines and destructive weapons'. For Lethbridge the similarity between such craft and the UFOs of modern reports was obvious and led to an inevitable conclusion about the 'sons of God'. Not without a note of embarrassment, he suggested that the myths were memories of extra-terrestrial visitations, and that 'perhaps five thousand or more years ago' beings from another world arrived here and thrust mankind a rung or two up the ladder of civilisation by contact and interbreeding.

Such ideas were not new, of course, although Lethbridge arrived at them independently. In 1968, just as he was completing his

Fit for heroes

Devotees of the ancient astronaut theory are fond of quoting the myths and legends of ancient or primitive peoples in an attempt to justify their case. The gods gave fire to mankind, and the skills of agriculture, according to the mythology of many peoples. But that does not mean that the gods arrived here in space ships – or even that humanity is so simple minded that it could not discover these things for itself. Not only that – ancient astronaut buffs seem not to have noticed a tendency in all mythology to describe the deeds and misdeeds of *heroic* figures.

Such people are believed to live grander, more expansive, slightly more real lives than do common mortals. The modern mythology of television soap opera likewise exaggerates its characters, simplifying the complexities of life to let us see them (and ourselves) more clearly – and so cope with them. Myths and legends also deal with deeply shocking events, but because they are inflicted on people slightly removed from the rest of us we can contemplate such actions with greater calm. And in this, perhaps, lies the secret of the gods and their gifts.

The discovery of fire must have been an astonishing event, full of magic and terror. How else to deal with it but regard it as the property of the gods, which has to be stolen by a Prometheus, who is then cruelly punished? Similarly, one of the most profound changes in human life occurred with the development of agriculture, involving enormous psychological and social upheaval – for which no mere man would want to take responsibility. Safer, then, to say that this was a gift from on high – and, furthermore, if this were the gods' will, what man would venture to resist the change, enormous and shocking though it was?

Opposite: the goddesses Demeter and Persephone hand Triptolemus the gift of grain for mankind before sending him on his journey to Earth. This Greek vase, from the 5th century BC, shows Triptolemus on a winged chariot

Below right: Ezekiel's vision of God was a terrifying experience. In the midst of a fiery brightness the prophet saw winged creatures 'that had the likeness of a man' and who 'sparkled like the colour of burnished brass'. Above them was a throne and a man enveloped in flames: 'this was the appearance of the likeness of the glory of God'

manuscript, *Chariots of the gods?* by Swiss hotelier Erich von Däniken appeared. A string of writers had tackled the 'ancient astronauts' theme long before von Däniken's skilful self-publicising made him appear to be its originator. The 19th-century occultist Helena Blavatsky had claimed that civilisation, if not mankind itself, had originated on another planet. And the mythological and anthropological evidence that von Däniken used to win fame and fortune had been carefully collected by a number of other researchers from the 1940s, most notably the Frenchmen Louis Pauwels and Jacques Bergier and the English writers Raymond Drake, John Michell and Brinsley le Poer Trench (who as Lord Clancarty instigated a debate on UFOs in the House of Lords in 1979).

Together, these writers have accumulated a mass of evidence (of varying quality) from the traditions and beliefs of every corner of

According to the Aborigines of Australia, beings known as the Wondjina (above) created the world and brought order out of chaos. The Wondjina are believed, by some Aborigines, to visit Earth in UFOs

Above: the earliest Hebrew coin, which dates from the 4th century BC, shows Jehovah seated on a winged chariot that resembles the chariot of Triptolemus on the Greek vase opposite. 'Was God an astronaut?' asked Erich von Däniken in the sub-title to his book *Chariots of the gods?*

Left: the Babylonians told of special beings who taught Man practical and artistic skills. These creatures were depicted with fish-tails, as is the goddess on this bronze monument

the globe, that forms an intriguing picture of evidence for extra-terrestrial intervention in Man's history. Most compelling of all are the ubiquitous myths of 'culture heroes' of mysterious origin who allegedly taught Man all the civilised arts. In the words of Lethbridge:

So many legends affirm that such and such a god taught mankind such and such an art. Hu the Mighty, for instance, so the Welsh Barddas say, taught men agriculture. Man did not evolve it by himself by painfully scratching with a pointed stick in the ground: a god taught him.

Many of these 'culture hero' legends seem to provide striking confirmation of the 'ancient astronaut' theory. The Babylonians preserved the story of a race of fish-tailed beings who rose every day from the Persian Gulf to teach their ancestors all the arts and sciences. They are paralleled in Greek myth by the amphibious gods called Telchines who spread metallurgical skills. Similar fish-beings called the Nommo are said by the Dogon tribe of West Africa to have descended from the skies in a whirling, thunderous craft. The Dogon attribute their civilisation to these beings, and their traditions about the invisible star Sirius B (home of the Nommo) display an alarming accuracy that has made the 'Sirius mystery' into one of the strongest arguments for extra-terrestrial contact in the long-forgotten past. Australian Aborigines attribute the creation and ordering of the world to beings known as the Wondjina. They preserve rock paintings of the Wondjina, and believe that these beings reside in the mysterious lights in the sky that white Australians call UFOs.

The culture bringers of these myths make particularly plausible 'extra-terrestrials' when they are associated with flying craft.

Like the ancient Welsh, the Greeks believed that agriculture was introduced rather than invented. The goddess Demeter sent her protegé Triptolemus around the world in a flying chariot with winged wheels, drawn by dragons, to distribute grain and teach agriculture and bread-making to all the world. Vase paintings show him perched on a chariot with two wheels, surmounted with wings and serpents. One is automatically reminded of the prophet Ezekiel's famous 'vision of God' that takes pride of place in so many 'ancient astronaut' books. Sitting by the river Chebar in Babylonia, Ezekiel saw a 'whirlwind' approach from the distance and turn into a fiery cloud, and then land with a noise like thunder. He was confronted with a dazzling vehicle that appeared to him to be composed of wheels, wings and living creatures. It carried a throne on which was seated 'a form in human likeness'. The similarity to the flying chariot of Triptolemus cannot be

accidental – a Jewish coin dating from the 4th century BC shows Jehovah seated on a vehicle similar to that of his Greek counterpart.

But the best mythology for the believer in extra-terrestrial intervention must be that of India. Its picturesque tales incorporate nearly all the essential elements of the other 'sons of God' legends. Gods and demi-gods descend from heaven, spreading knowledge and taking mortal women as their wives. They fly on strange beasts or magnificent craft that can leave the wind behind. The epics describe aerial battles involving lightning-like missiles that can turn countryside into wasteland. One such weapon contains the Power of the Universe and unleashes 'smoke brighter than ten thousand suns'. According to writers like Raymond Drake and Erich von Däniken all one needs to do is read 'extra-terrestrials' for 'gods' and the Indian legends are revealed as a *Star wars*-style history of ancient astronautics.

As the ancient astronaut writers pile on story after story of sky gods, culture heroes, flying chariots and the like, the idea that extra-terrestrials were somehow behind it all begins to seem like an almost natural explanation. The idea is sufficiently intriguing to create a demand for 'hard' proof. Or disproof. We should be careful of trying to explain one unknown, such as the legend of 'the sons of God', by putting forward another unknown, extra-terrestrial life. The mythological picture on its own is merely suggestive, a possible pointer to an uncharted area of human history. The legends of Homer were vindicated many centuries later when archaeologist Heinrich Schliemann uncovered the ruins of Troy and Mycenae – but have the 'space gods' yet found their Schliemann?

Erich von Däniken startled the world and gained international fame by suggesting that superior space-beings visited Earth in ancient times. But how much credence do his views really deserve?

ALL GENUINE MYTHS contain a kernel of truth. It might be a human psychological yearning for some higher state, as in the myths of the 'Superman'. Or it might be an indication of the importance, no longer understood, once attached to some special place such as a megalithic site. Other myths reflect memories of historical events and people, like King Arthur or the Emperor Charlemagne. Some may even take us a surprising way back into prehistory. The North American Indian stories concerning the time when their world was dominated by the 'Big Snow' sound like a description of the last ice age, which ended 10,000 years ago.

But how do we understand those myths that read like pure fiction, yet occur in slightly different versions in the traditions of ancient peoples and tribal cultures from widely separated parts of the globe? They include the stories of the 'gods', or 'sky people', or beings from stars, who came down to Earth and civilised mankind (see page 83). They flew, we are sometimes told, in winged or fiery chariots, and a few select mortals were given rides or carried off in them. These visitors from 'heaven' were even supposed to have taken human partners, breeding demigods who became kings and wisemen. So where did *these* stories come from? Should we try to explain them, like beliefs in the afterlife, in terms of Man's psychological needs? Or are we missing the point if we do not give these myths a chance and try to interpret them at their face value?

A possible explanation

Many people believe that with the benefit of 20th-century scientific knowledge we can now understand such myths in ways that simply were not available to scholars of previous centuries. Today, the possibility (at least) of extra-terrestrial life-forms is one that most people are happy to entertain. As Man begins the long trek into the solar system and the investigation of other worlds, the question of whether our own planet has been already visited by some other intelligent life-form has arisen quite naturally. Could the idea of the 'gods from heaven' be ancient Man's attempt to describe his own experience of beings from other worlds, in the days before it was really known that such worlds existed? And wouldn't tales of fiery chariots that flew through the air be the only way that ancient Man could describe the kinds of air and space travel we now know to be possible?

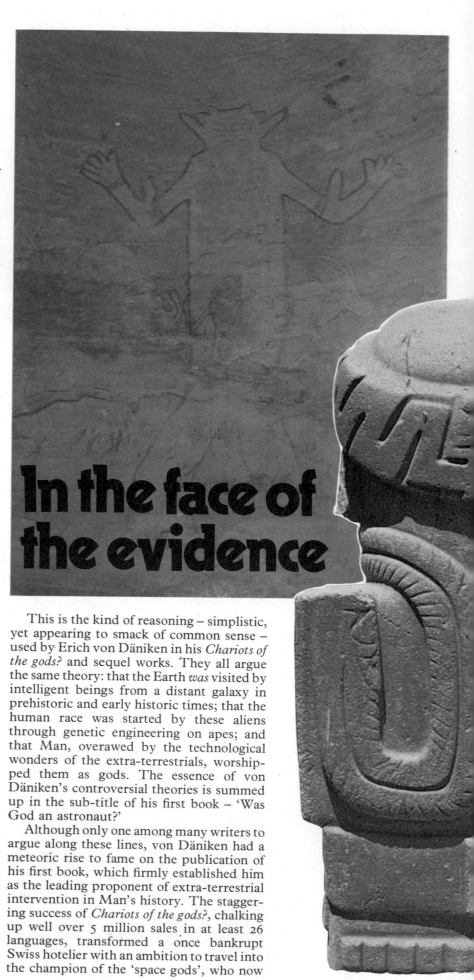

In the face of the evidence

This is the kind of reasoning – simplistic, yet appearing to smack of common sense – used by Erich von Däniken in his *Chariots of the gods?* and sequel works. They all argue the same theory: that the Earth *was* visited by intelligent beings from a distant galaxy in prehistoric and early historic times; that the human race was started by these aliens through genetic engineering on apes; and that Man, overawed by the technological wonders of the extra-terrestrials, worshipped them as gods. The essence of von Däniken's controversial theories is summed up in the sub-title of his first book – 'Was God an astronaut?'

Although only one among many writers to argue along these lines, von Däniken had a meteoric rise to fame on the publication of his first book, which firmly established him as the leading proponent of extra-terrestrial intervention in Man's history. The staggering success of *Chariots of the gods?*, chalking up well over 5 million sales in at least 26 languages, transformed a once bankrupt Swiss hotelier with an ambition to travel into the champion of the 'space gods', who now

Left: for von Däniken, this intriguing figure from a rock painting in the Tassili mountains of Algeria depicts a spaceman making a visit to Earth centuries ago. The ethereal form contrasts with the more solid drawings in the group

At Tiahuanaco, Bolivia, impressive sculptures and monuments (below and below right) proclaim stupendous building feats by ancient Man – or are they the result of extra-terrestrial intervention?

pursues his quest for 'final proof' around the globe with an almost messianic zeal. His success is particularly amazing as hardly a single thought contained in his books is original. Every link in the von Däniken argument can be found in the work of earlier, often far sounder, exponents of the 'ancient astronaut' theme. Archaeologists and theologians reacted with outrage, however, denouncing him as a fraud and a charlatan.

Von Däniken assures us that he has plenty of 'hard proof' that extra-terrestrials have visited and 'deposited physical signs of their presence on Earth'. He crams his books with details of ancient artefacts claimed to be representations of spacemen, rockets, aerials, and even heart-transplants, and describes feats of engineering that 'couldn't possibly' have been managed by ancient Man without 'outside help'.

But most of his evidence is a mish-mash of half-truths, cooked up with insinuations made in the form of questions. The argument is sometimes so thin that von Däniken has used the vagueness of his own question-without-answer style of writing to wriggle on the hook when critics have caught him out. The famous ground drawings of animals at Nazca in Peru were described by him in *Chariots of the gods?* as follows: 'Seen from the air, the clear-cut impression that the . . . plain of Nazca made on *me* was that of an airfield!' And his other comments make it perfectly clear that this is what he wants the reader to believe. The real nature of the Nazca lines has been studied at first hand since the 1940s by the German scientist Maria Reiche, who has not found the slightest trace of extra-terrestrial landings. At the mention of von Däniken's airstrips, she smiled and remarked: 'Once you remove the

stones, the ground is quite soft. I'm afraid the spacemen would have gotten stuck.'

In a debate with a sceptical Colin Wilson in the magazine *Second Look* (January 1979), von Däniken tried to soft-pedal on the question of the Nazca lines: 'I have not claimed that extra-terrestrials had built the lines at Nazca. I have only said these tracks were the result of some sort of cargo-cult of the natives there.' He challenged Wilson to produce a statement from one of his books to the effect that the lines were built 'by or with the help of extra-terrestrials'. On Wilson's behalf, here is an extract from von Däniken's *Return to the stars*:

At some time in the past, unknown intelligences landed on the uninhabited plain near the present-day town of Nazca and built an improvised airfield for their spacecraft which were to operate in the vicinity of the earth. They laid down two runways on the ideal terrain.

And in *Chariots of the gods?* von Däniken claimed that the lines in general 'could also have been built according to instructions from an aircraft'.

He has been forced to back down on many other points. With regard to the non-rusting, welded-together pillar at Meharauli, India which he misdated and wrongly described, he later admitted in an interview in *Playboy* magazine:

. . . when I wrote *Chariots of the gods?* the information I had concerning this iron column was as I presented it. Since then, I have found that investigations were made and they came to quite different results, so we can forget about this iron thing.

Another classic case is the question of the

Däniken said he 'felt tremendously happy', though he 'had the feeling of being constantly watched'.

This 'expedition' to the Ecuadorean tunnels became the subject of a farcical controversy between von Däniken and Juan Moricz. Four months after the publication of *The gold of the gods*, von Däniken admitted to two editors of *Der Spiegel* that he had never been to the part of Ecuador in question, though he had done some underground exploring 60 miles (100 kilometres) away near the town of Cuenca. And in his *Playboy* interview he admitted that the dramatic details of his adventures in the tunnels were largely imaginary, but excusable on grounds of 'author's licence'. Meanwhile, Moricz stated categorically in an interview that 'Däniken never set foot in the caves. . . . If he

secret system of tunnels beneath the mountains of Ecuador, containing mysterious treasures of prehistoric artefacts and a 'library' of metal plates inscribed with records of a visit by 'space gods'; a description of these supposed relics forms the centrepiece of von Däniken's *The gold of the gods* (1970). He claims to have explored this vast underground network with the help of Juan Moricz, self-styled discoverer and 'keeper' of the tunnels. He described his experiences in graphic detail:

> . . . we switched on our torches and the lamps on our helmets, and there in front of us was the gaping hole which led down into the depths. . . . We slid down a rope to the first platform.

As he marvelled at the wonders contained in the tunnels, such as the metal plates covered with a bizarre and unknown script, von

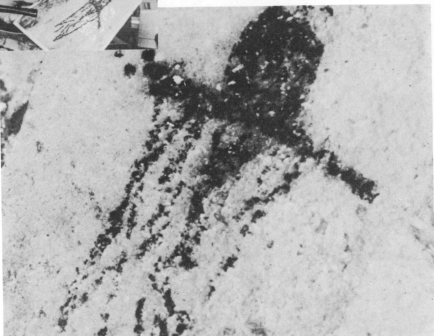

Top: Erich von Däniken, most celebrated of the 'ancient astronaut' theorists

Above: this cave drawing from Soledad in the Baja peninsula of Mexico is said to show a flying saucer belching flames from its underside. Does it constitute 'evidence' of a visiting spacecraft in ancient times?

Left: the candelabra 'tree of life' above Pisco in Peru is a mysterious set of lines that some people say point towards Nazca, about 120 miles (190 kilometres) away. One view is that it is a 19th-century navigational aid

says he personally saw the library and the other things, he's lying.' Moricz claims to have merely shown von Däniken a side-entrance to the tunnel network: 'You couldn't enter the cave, though, it's blocked.' As for the treasures, Moricz says these were photographed by von Däniken in a local museum, 'but most of the contents are junk'.

Moricz himself is an ambiguous character: his 'ownership' of the tunnels has been disputed, and no reputable archaeologist or geologist has seemingly been allowed anywhere near the mysterious caverns containing the library, which he continues to claim are genuine. Though he states he showed nothing of importance to von Däniken, Moricz began legal proceedings against him, demanding a percentage of von Däniken's royalties for illegally publicising his own discoveries.

Despite his previous admissions, von Däniken still claimed in the *Second Look* article: 'What I have said in *The gold of the gods* about these underground caves is all true.' He insists that he saw the metal library with his own eyes and, according to his biographer Peter Krassa, he knows intuitively that the tunnels contain *the* proof of his theories.

Paucity of evidence

Despite the claims put forward in *The gold of the gods*, and in numerous interviews and articles, no one has yet produced the slightest scrap of evidence that there is anything 'extra-terrestrial' about the supposed discoveries. Even if the tunnels are artificial – though a local geological authority thinks they are natural formations – and even if they do contain gold objects and a 'mysterious' library with an undeciphered script, so what? How do the 'ancient astronauts' benefit from all this? Von Däniken repeated Moricz's assertion that the library 'might contain a synopsis of the history of humanity, as well as an account of the origin of mankind on earth and information about a vanished civilisation'. But neither von Däniken nor Moricz claims to have deciphered a single letter of the script. And far from producing any relics manufactured by an unknown alien race, all the objects that they display as spoils of the caves are rather unsophisticated-looking objects of tin and brass (not gold) that could be made by any competent smith. Yet *The gold of the gods* announces the evidence from the tunnels as 'the most incredible, fantastic story of the century'.

Small wonder, then, that von Däniken's critics have often labelled him a fraud. But despite the numerous instances where von Däniken has been shown to have fudged his facts, sometimes on his own admission, millions of his readers still feel convinced by the bulk of the evidence in *Chariots of the gods?*, and the similar arguments put forward by other writers in books like it. What about the Piri Re'is and other Renaissance maps that

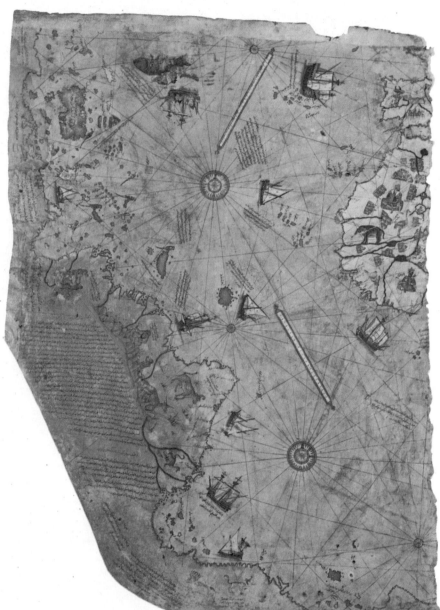

Above: the Piri Re'is map, dated 1513, is said by von Däniken to show mountains in Antarctica – centuries before they were discovered by Europeans – buried deep under snow and ice. Von Däniken says the map is based on aerial photographs. Cartographers have pointed out that the map holds few mysteries and is a noticeably inaccurate compilation of several different charts

Left: the lines at Nazca, Peru, a focus of controversy in the debate about visitations to Earth by beings from space

apparently show details of the Antarctic continent now covered by thick layers of ice? What about the incredible building feats such as the pyramids of Egypt, Tiahuanaco in Bolivia, Sacsayhuaman in Peru and the huge idols of Easter Island? Or the electric dry batteries and crystal lenses from ancient Mesopotamia, the intricate astronomical calculator found off the coast of Greece at Antikythera, or the massive stone spheres of almost perfect construction scattered in the dense jungles and forests of Costa Rica? Von Däniken may have made crass mistakes, but don't the mythologies of the world suggest that 'gods' did once visit the Earth? Might not such a list of technological feats, almost unimaginable as the products of ancient Man, prove that extra-terrestrial intelligence *was* once at work on our planet?

No time like the present

Those who believe that space-beings visited Earth centuries ago point to wonders of the ancient world as evidence of extra-terrestrial achievement. But were ancient peoples really incapable of such accomplishments?

WHILE MOST ARCHAEOLOGICAL WORK is concerned with the mundane bric-a-brac and rubbish left by ancient societies, every now and again an object turns up that completely surpasses all previous estimates of an ancient culture's technical skill. During the 1970s archaeologists working in Bulgaria made an extraordinary series of discoveries about the Neolithic Karanovo culture that flourished there around 4500 BC. The finds date from a time when Man is generally thought to have had little or no knowledge of metallurgy – yet the Karanovo graves revealed a surprising treasure-trove of beautiful finely made gold and copper jewellery and weapons. Finds such as these are slowly, but continually, forcing archaeologists to reassess their views of ancient Man's technological abilities.

Egypt has produced more scientific wonders, often of great antiquity, than any other region. The ancient Egyptians had an advanced knowledge of medicine and surgery. They knew sufficient to use contraceptives of honey and acacia gum (an effective spermicide), and it has even been suggested that they understood the use of penicillin. A model wooden glider of around 200 BC from Saqqara shows a surprisingly accurate basic grasp of the principles of aerodynamics. And the Great Pyramid, built around 2600 BC, amazes even 20th-century Man with its sheer size and the beauty of its architectural perfection.

Many writers have insisted that the Great Pyramid of Cheops at Gîza could not be built even with present-day scientific skill and machinery. Erich von Däniken, for one, stated bluntly in *Chariots of the gods?*: 'Today, in the twentieth century, no architect could build a copy of the Pyramid of Cheops, even if the technical resources of

Left: the façade of the tomb of Sneferu, with the Great Pyramid of Cheops behind. Erich von Däniken gives the weight of the pyramid as more than 31 million tonnes and says it would have taken ordinary mortals 664 years to build. In fact the pyramid weighs about 6 million tonnes, and engineers and archaeologists estimate that it could have been erected well within the 23-year reign of its builder, Cheops

Below left: a Persian frieze showing archers, dating from the sixth century BC. Many technological secrets of ancient glazing were 'lost' during the Dark Ages and were rediscovered in western Europe only during the industrial revolution

Were the gods worshipped by ancient Man really interplanetary visitors? Marduk, god of agriculture, is shown on a seal (right) from Mesopotamia, dating from the third century BC. The head of an idol (below) is from Bulgaria, where a very advanced culture existed as long ago as the fifth millennium BC

every continent were at his disposal.' The implication of such a claim is obvious: if *we* couldn't build it, how could the ancient Egyptians have done so with their basic technology and simple tools? Did the Egyptians have 'outside help', from extra-terrestrial intelligence?

Von Däniken and other supporters of the 'ancient astronaut' theory draw similar conclusions for many of the architectural wonders of the ancient world. Another puzzling structure often cited is the huge stone complex of Tiahuanaco, near Lake Titicaca in the high Andes mountains of Bolivia. Added to these architectural feats is an increasing list of technological 'ancient anomalies', many of which have been discussed in the pages of *The Unexplained*. Taken together, the file suggests that much of the advanced knowledge we proudly believe is peculiar to our modern world may have been available hundreds, even thousands, of years ago – including sophisticated metallurgy, surgical operations, the use of electricity and the idea of heavier-than-air flight. If we also take into account the myths of the 'gods' who taught Man the arts and sciences, then the case for extra-terrestrial intervention in Man's early history almost begins to look plausible.

But is the extra-terrestrial hypothesis really a fair explanation of ancient technological 'anomalies'? Unfortunately, writers like von Däniken too often exaggerate and distort the evidence. And in order to show that extra-terrestrial help was needed, von Däniken has to attempt to discredit the Egyptians by implying that they had none of the basic resources necessary for such a massive undertaking as the construction of the Great Pyramid.

Almost every stage of von Däniken's argument relies on a misinterpretation of the facts, and the clear evidence that the Egyptians themselves were responsible for the Great Pyramid is ignored or brushed aside. The fact is that the name of Pharaoh Cheops (or Khufu), remembered by the later Egyptians as the cruel taskmaster who had ordered the building of the Great Pyramid, is carved on some of its limestone blocks. The structure *is* an extraordinary achievement, but the Egyptians were, without doubt, masters of mathematics, architecture, stone-masonry and, above all, organisation. The dozens of other pyramids dotted along the Nile Valley, ranging from a few feet high to little short of the Great Pyramid's 450 feet (137 metres), stand as witnesses to the fact that Egyptians could have built Cheops's pyramid.

A false impression

Cheops's Great Pyramid and other 'ancient anomalies' can only be made into extra-terrestrial artefacts at the expense of ancient peoples. By creaming off their greatest achievements as 'proof' of extra-terrestrial intervention, von Däniken creates a false impression that is downright insulting to highly sophisticated ancient cultures like those of the Egyptians, Mayans, Hindus and Babylonians. Carl Sagan summed up: 'Essentially, von Däniken's argument is that our ancestors were too stupid to create the most impressive surviving architectural and artistic works.'

Archaeological evidence, often just shards and fragments, is far too limited to reconstruct the real scope of ancient peoples' skill and knowledge. We would not like to be assessed by soft-drink bottles, which will far outlast the paper on which are described our educational systems, the thoughts of our philosophers and saints, our medical knowledge and the mathematics and scientific skills that have flown us to the nearest planets. Nor would we like to think that an archaeologist of the future would ascribe the remains of a fragmentary radio, preserved by chance conditions, to an alien intelligence. Yet this is how von Däniken treats the evidence that indicates ancient Man may have used surprisingly advanced technology.

The ancient astronaut theorists, while professing to be free-thinking and far-sighted, are actually the victims of a very narrow view of history that sees our own era as the most important point in time, a focus by which all other historical periods must be evaluated. Books like *Chariots of the gods?* ooze enthusiasm for the scientific know-how of the space age. Von Däniken wrote his first books for a public fully charged with excitement by the Apollo space probes, which culminated in the first manned landing on the Moon in 1969 – the proof that interplanetary travel was possible. For von Däniken, Man's history is seen solely in terms of a development from 'primitive' ancestors to the present stage of space-age technology. He zealously seeks spacesuits, goggles, lunar modules and the other trappings of space-age technology in ancient art – as if beings capable of crossing the vast distances of interstellar space would be using anything like the crude equipment we use to reach the Moon! Many skills and techniques that once flourished are now forgotten, and many discoveries are simply rediscoveries of knowledge that has faded away or been obliterated by man-made and natural destruction. We should avoid the all too easy mistake of thinking that the scientists of the modern world are the only kind of people capable of advanced technological feats.

The ancient astronaut school's interpretation of mythology fails because of this narrow view of history. It compares myths of flying chariots and helpful gods from heaven

Above right: 'Behold, there appeared a chariot of fire . . . and Elijah went up by a whirlwind into heaven.' The fiery chariot is not meant to be taken literally. In the story of Elijah it provides a graphic means of describing death

Right: Krishna, on the bird-god Garuda, fights Indra, seated on an elephant. In Hindu legend, Krishna performed miracles, subdued Indra and slew Kamsa, usurper of the throne of Mathura. For 'ancient astronaut' theorists, such legends indicate that extra-terrestrial beings visited Earth long ago

Far right: part of the famous Inca fortress at Sacsahuaman, Peru, which testifies to ancient Man's technical skills

with the 20th-century concepts of space flight and extra-terrestrial intelligences. We are asked to leap back in time with the image of the modern astronaut into the world of the Greek and Egyptian gods. But what about the centuries in between? Did the 'space gods' suddenly disappear from Man's mythology? A fact ignored by von Däniken is that they did not. All the motifs in the 'legends of the sons of God' that are used to argue the case for extra-terrestrial intervention in ancient times continue to be found much later, not only in the stories collected by anthropologists, but in the extensive fairy-lore of medieval and post-medieval Europe. They include the appearance of supernatural deities in mysterious flying craft, the abduction of mortals to remote worlds, and the superior knowledge of the strange visitors, usually benign, who teach selected mortals new skills and arts.

A legend often cited by the ancient astronaut lobby is the North American Indian

tale of the adventures of Algon or Wampee:
> Wampee was hunting one day when he came across a circular depression on a clearing of rich grass. Hearing the strains of distant music he looked up and saw a speck in the sky; the speck drew nearer and nearer, and proved to be a basket, which came to ground on the circle marked on the grass. From it stepped twelve beautiful maidens. When they began to dance, Wampee, overcome with passion, ran into the clearing, but when they saw him they resumed their song and the basket carried them off into the sky. Wampee returned to the clearing frequently, and one day he managed to capture one of the maidens, making her his wife. She bore him a son, but missing her own kind she built a circular basket and flew away from the earth with her son, never to be seen again.

Is this myth really a memory of an ancient extra-terrestrial contact, when it is such a close parallel to the tales of meetings with 'elfin' people still reported until this century in the remoter corners of the British Isles? And the resemblance to some of the more bizarre UFO stories of today is striking.

In fact, a comparison of the myths that supposedly describe extra-terrestrial visitations, medieval and modern fairy-lore, and the more exotic UFO contact stories, shows that they are certainly part and parcel of the same phenomenon. (John Michell has amply demonstrated this point in *The flying saucer vision*.) There are many people alive today who claim to have 'seen' the fairy world or to have flown in a flying saucer. While they probably had *some* kind of experience, no one would take their stories literally. Yet von Däniken takes at face value an ancient myth about a romance between a mortal and a god and offers it as 'evidence' that aliens have

Above: a 19th-century illustration of elfin cruelty. In the realm of the imagination anything is possible – and folklore includes many stories that are similar to modern-day UFO sightings

genetically manipulated Man's evolution. While he mentions UFO sightings, von Däniken ignores the bizarre UFO *contact* stories and the medieval fairy-lore. Yet the myths of 'space gods' that he uses as main evidence have the appearance of ancient UFO contact stories. The medieval fairy-lore is a vital 'missing link' that bridges the gap between the two kinds of story. The 'little green men' of modern UFO mythology are unmistakably the green-clad elves of Celtic folklore.

A product of the mind?

For many years it was standard to view the UFO phenomenon simply in terms of extra-terrestrial craft, an interpretation now on the wane. While many UFO sightings may be of 'hardware' of some sort, this theory does not explain the contact stories, a phenomenon that is at least half in the mind. Just as von Däniken sees ancient art in terms of space-suits and lunar modules, so the observer of a 'UFO landing' seems to interpret the experience through his own cultural filter and 'see' a fiery chariot, fairy ship or spacecraft, depending on the age he lives in. There are too many such stories to doubt that the phenomenon is real, whether it belongs to an entirely psychological world or to physical realities normally out of our reach. Possibly it borrows from both, but the interpretation in terms of rocket packs or gossamer wings is certainly a subjective product of the contactee.

Trying to understand the psychology behind the whole range of stories of Man's contact with 'other beings' is a less easy, perhaps less satisfying, approach than the glib 'spaceman' theories of the ancient astronaut school. But it will tell us far more about the human mind and its attempts to come to terms with the unknown. Rather than force the ancient gods into the strait-jackets of 'ancient astronauts', we should instead use mythology and folklore to help us gain a wider perspective on modern stories of close encounters with 'extra-terrestrials'.

Index